The Crux of the Matter

The Crux of the Matter

A Study of the Cross

David Whitaker

The Crux of the Matter: A Study of the Cross

Unless otherwise noted, all scriptural references herein are taken from the Authorized King James Version of the Bible.

FOR INFORMATION CONTACT:
David Whitaker
www.hopetabernacle.com

Contents

Chapter One

The Crux of the Matter

Then said Jesus unto the twelve, Will ye also go away? Then Simon Peter answered him, Lord, to whom shall we go? thou hast the words of eternal life (John 6:67-68).

crux (kruks) *n. pl.* **cruxes** or **cruces** (kroo'sez).

1. A pivotal, fundamental, or vital point.
2. A cross.
3. A tormenting or baffling problem. [< L. *cross*]

(Funk & Wagnalls Standard Desk Dictionary Vol. 1, 1964)

The "crux of the matter" is a term used to describe the center point of a subject or the central meaning and origin of a particular concept. The word *crux* gets its origins from the Latin word meaning "cross."

If you look at Christianity as a whole—the entire existence of the New Testament church and everything it may involve—you will not have to go very far in study to discover that the crux of the matter is, without question or debate, the cross. Even if you take the Bible as a whole, from Genesis to Revelation, you will discover that the fundamental, vital point is the cross. I know that the cross was not physically noted until the actual time of Christ, but if we go back to the book of beginnings we read:

> *And I will put enmity between thee and the woman, and between thy seed and her seed; it shall bruise thy head, and thou shalt bruise his heel* (Genesis 3:15).

As early as the third chapter of Genesis, we see the first prophecy about the promise of victory over Satan at the cross. In fact, every verse of Scripture that follows Genesis 3:15 is a fulfillment of that one prophecy.

Think about it. . . . Every story, every event that took place for four thousand years led to Calvary. Every type and every shadow leads us to the crux of the matter, which is the cross. This is why Paul told Galatia that the Old Testament is our schoolmaster that leads us to Christ (Galatians 3:24).

Peter wrote:

> *But with the precious blood of Christ, as of a lamb without blemish and without spot: who verily was foreordained before the foundation of the world, but was manifest in these last times for you* (I Peter 1:19-20).

John wrote in Revelation 13:8b, "the Lamb slain from the foundation of the world." The Lamb that was slain was Jesus Christ, the Lamb of God. The cross was in the plan of God from the very beginning.

The apostle John told us again in his Gospel that the Word (*Gr. Logos*, meaning plan or concept) of God was in the beginning with God, and that plan was made flesh (born in the physical body of Jesus Christ) and lived among us (John 1:1-14). The plan of God, from the beginning, was to create a man who would replace the Tabernacle of the Old Testament and become a human temple to house the Spirit of the one true and living God. And that plan "became flesh, and did tabernacle among us" (John 1:14, *Young's Literal Translation*). This human tabernacle, God in flesh, would become the holy sacrifice and ultimately die for the sins of all mankind. Calvary was ordained of God, and nothing could have stopped Jesus from being crucified. No power on earth, no chance of circumstance, no outcome of fate could have altered the Day of Atonement at Calvary.

In Genesis 12 we read about a man who was called from the land of the Chaldeans, to leave the city of Ur and to journey to the Land of Promise. Abraham was on a mission to establish a people and a country so that there could be a capital city. In this city God would cause His name to dwell (Deuteronomy 12:11). Just outside the city would stand a mountain called Calvary. Why was this necessary? Because God's plan (the *logos*) was being executed.

A throne needed to be established for a king to reign, so in Exodus God released the children of Israel from the bondage of Egypt and sent them back to the land of promise. They too were on a mission, to drive out the inhabitants of the land and to prepare a place for the king.

The prophet Samuel was born for the purpose of anointing the king of Israel. This king, named David, would establish a throne and the city that would be prepared for his descendant . . . the real King of Israel, none other than Jesus himself (Isaiah 9:7).

You can read from one chapter to the next, from Genesis to Malachi, and you will quickly realize that everything leads us to the cross. All the great patriarchs of old were in fact on a mission. They all journeyed in faith and obeyed without wavering, to help fulfill a promise that they never would behold with mortal eyes.

> *And what shall I more say? for the time would fail me to tell of Gedeon, and of Barak, and of Samson, and of Jephthae; of David also, and Samuel, and of the prophets* (Hebrews 11:32).

These all lived and died to bring us to a precious promise. The writer of the Book of Hebrews spent much time explaining how we came from the law to the cross (Hebrews 1-10). These passages describe how the death and the resurrection of Christ were shadowed in the mosaic law. Then, we read that great men and women of faith were commissioned by God to journey toward a promise, from Abel to Noah, Abraham to Moses, and David to the last Old Testament prophets. That promise was the cross. This great mystery of old has now been revealed to us by way of the death, burial, and resurrection of Jesus Christ our Lord (I Timothy 3:16).

When Pilate declared to Jesus, "Knowest thou not that I have power to crucify thee, and have power to release thee?" (John 19:10), he had no idea that every event in the past four thousand years was leading up to this moment in time.

I love the response of Jesus when He replied, "Thou couldest have no power at all against me, except it were given thee from above" (John 19:11). No power on earth could have altered Calvary. The cross had to happen.

As we understand that every event prior to the cross led to us to the cross, we cannot think that the cross is now behind us and we are somehow beyond its relevance in our lives. J. T. Pugh described this:

> True Christianity is always a present experience. It is never meant to be historical only. . . . The "slaying of the lamb" in principle began in the garden of Eden so that man's and woman's nakedness might be covered

(Genesis 3:21). Peter shows that redemption was in the foreknowledge of God, "before the foundation of the world" (1 Peter 1:19). . . . The Lamb was slain in the offering of Isaac, in the martyrdom of James, and in the death of countless lambs for 1,739 years (Scoffield Chronology).

This principle of vicarious suffering continues with the church. Paul described himself as "always bearing about the body of the dying of the Lord Jesus" (2 Cor 4:10). This was the basic Christian attitude of the apostle Paul. This was his approach to life. In this standard Christian lifestyle, the cross principle was the continual guide.

"The dying of the Lord Jesus" was evident in Paul's verbal ministry to the Corinthians. The shadow of the cross always fell across his teaching sessions. "And I, brethren, when I came to you, came not with excellency of speech or of wisdom, declaring unto you the testimony of God. For I determined not to know anything among you, save Jesus Christ and him crucified. And I was with you in weakness, and in fear, and in much trembling. And my speech and my preaching was not with enciting words of man's wisdom, but in demonstration of the Spirit and of power; that your faith should not stand in the wisdom of men, but in the power of God" (1 Cor 2: 1-5).[1]

---

[1] *The Wisdom and the Power of the Cross*, J. T. Pugh. Copyright 1998.

We know that Jesus died on the cross over two thousand years ago; however, the cross should never be viewed as a past event. It is just as relevant to our daily lives as it was for those present on the day it occurred. The cross is present at every meeting of Christians; every time a sinner repents, he is at the cross. Every time someone is healed of a disease or delivered of a drug addiction, baptized in the water and filled with the Holy Spirit, the cross is just as relevant as it was. The effect of Calvary will never lose its efficacy, it will never lose its relativity, it will never get outdated, and it will never become simply a historical event. Paul spoke of the cross as an ongoing event. "As it is written, For thy sake we are killed all the day long; we are accounted as sheep for the slaughter" (Romans 8:36).

Jesus told us that we cannot even look to the future without first looking back to the cross. In His instructions at the Last Supper, Jesus said that we should eat the bread that represents His broken body and drink the wine that represents His shed blood. "This do in remembrance of me" (Luke 22:19). Paul likewise quoted this passage and then added, "For as often as you eat this bread and drink this cup, you proclaim the Lord's death till He comes" (I Corinthians 11:26, NKJV). The Christian hope is birthed in our faith of the second coming of Jesus Christ. However, we cannot even look toward our hope without proclaiming the cross. Paul told the church to proclaim the cross until He comes.

Paul further added:

> *And I, brethren, when I came to you, came not with excellency of speech or of wisdom, declaring unto you the testimony of God. For I determined not to know any thing among you, save Jesus Christ, and him crucified* (I Corinthians 2:1-2).

Paul declared nothing to them except the cross of Jesus. What do you know, Paul? "Nothing but the cross." The cross is the heart of the entire matter. It is the crux of our faith, the center of our salvation, and the heart of the message.

The Book of Revelation is none other than the "Revelation of Jesus Christ." No one can have a revelation of Jesus without recognizing the cross. In this book, John was shown many things about the future of the church. He saw the Lord Jesus as the King of kings and the Lord of lords (Revelation 19:16). He was given insight to the throne of God and saw one sitting upon that throne. That one is Jesus (Revelation 5:6). John observed the victorious King and the all-sovereign God, but you will notice very quickly that John's heavenly vision was not without the presence of the cross.

Even as John saw the Lord on the throne, he described Him this way: "a Lamb as it had been slain" (Revelation 5:6). The term "lamb" indicates the moment that Jesus was sacrificed as the Lamb of God on the cross. The term John used "as it had been slain" indicates a detail of how Jesus looked in these instances—Jesus as He had been crucified. John was shown the victorious future of the church and a great vision of the triumphant Lord and King but not without the bloody reminder of Calvary. In fact, John used the term "lamb" twenty-seven times in twenty-two verses of the Book of Revelation. It is almost as if God did not want John ever to forget the significance of the cross.

> *Behold, he cometh with clouds; and every eye shall see him, and they also which pierced him: and all kindreds of the earth shall wail because of him* (Revelation 1:7).

This verse does not refer to Jesus as the Lamb; however, it does tell us that all who see Him will remember the cross by way of His pierced hands and feet. As Jesus returns in great triumph and victory, we will all behold Him and will be reminded of the cross. The cross is in the past, yet it truly is ever before us. No one will ever escape the reality of the cross (Philippians 2:10).

iLife

The setting of the text found at the beginning of this chapter is quite fitting in understanding the effect that Calvary should have upon each of us. "Then said Jesus unto the twelve, Will ye also go away? Then Simon Peter answered him, Lord, to whom shall we go? thou hast the words of eternal life" (John 6:67-68). The previous day, Jesus had performed the miracle of feeding the five thousand with five loaves and two fish (John 6:11). After the multitude witnessed the miracle, they approached Jesus and wanted to make Him King. Jesus, in turn, vanished until the next day. In John 6:22-68 the crowd found Jesus and began to ask Him to perform more miracles. What they actually wanted was more bread (John 6:26).

Here Jesus completed the lesson from the day before. He fed them in order to share with them some valuable truths that would ultimately thin the crowd from five thousand men plus women and children (approximately fourteen thousand people) to a mere twelve men. His message was this: the bread they sought was physical, but the bread they should really be seeking was eternal salvation through Jesus Christ alone. This heavenly bread was like the manna that came from heaven in the wilderness. Their fathers ate the bread from heaven, and it gave them physical nourishment and life.

Then Jesus moved into the hard teaching about the cross. Jesus declared that His body was like the manna from heaven, and whosoever would eat His flesh and drink His blood would have eternal life. You may notice the connection between this message and the one Jesus gave the disciples on the night of the Last Supper.

> *And he took bread, and gave thanks, and brake it, and gave unto them, saying, This is my body which is given for you: this do in remembrance of me. Likewise also the cup after supper, saying, This cup is the new testament in my blood, which is shed for you* (Luke 22:19-20).

This was not offensive to the men sitting with Jesus at the Last Supper. However, when Jesus addressed the crowd in John 6, they were quickly turned off. No one likes the thought of seeing a body broken into pieces and blood being poured out. Certainly, no one likes the thought of having to partake in the event of a bloody sacrifice. Jesus had many followers and many even called themselves His disciples, but the closer He drew to Calvary, the fewer and fewer His followers became. Jesus continued to weed out those who could not bear the reality that free food and blessings from God will always require a sacrifice. This was not a popular message then, and it is not a popular message today.

Our culture today is centered on the "me" concept. Apple Inc. has made sure we all live in the "I" world. Everything Apple produces taps into the heart of this culture, from the iPhone to the iMac. If you're going to get a tablet, you better get the iPad. (And there is nothing wrong with good marketing.) Apple realized the value our culture places on individuality and began to sell the "I" product. It is all about my-life and my-choice, my-idea, and my-truth. I am not an expert on this, but Steve Jobs did an incredible job developing a subculture of devices that cater to our newest philosophies.

As with many marketing platforms, this one happened totally by accident. The "I" originally intended to stand for internet, but it has become the new way for Apple to say "personal" or "custom fit for you."

This is "iTtunes" or my-music. Everything can be specific, custom catered for the user alone. This subculture has redefined our entertainment, our communication, and our way of life. This subculture has now become our main culture. Pandora radio has brought it to another level. You choose the radio station you want, and then as the songs play, you can hit the like button or the dislike button as you see fit. The more you listen, the more personal your radio station becomes. If you will notice, everything is moving in this direction.

Churches are no different. There are several different styles of worship and preaching. It seems that every church is developing and marketing itself to reach this "I" culture. People are given many choices, even within a single church building. Worship the way *you* want. The sign outside the church reads: 8AM Contemporary and 10AM Traditional. More and more churches are offering the public choices even in Sunday school classes. Show up at 10AM, and you choose the class that best fits you. There is nothing wrong with reaching our current culture or speaking their language. I merely point this out to prove a point about our culture today.

While it may be good to offer a selection of classes that best fits the needs of the individual, the problem is not with worship styles or allowance for options per se. However, we do hear more and more people saying things like, "I am looking for a church that fits my needs," or, "This church was good for a while, but I want something different now." I have even heard people say, "I want to take a break from church for a while." People want blessings without obligation. They want salvation, but they want choices in their salvation. This mind-set goes beyond a music style or what class may be most relevant to them. In fact, choices in worship, styles of music, and styles of preaching are taking precedence over truth. Just like the people in Jesus' day, they want their bread and they want it their way. They want the miracles, but they do not want a broken body and spilled blood. They want religion, but they do not want the cross.

The message of eating His flesh and drinking His blood is what repulsed the masses. Jesus was telling them, "The message that I preach is not like your Apple device." This is not iWord, iBible, iPastor, iLife, and most certainly not iJesus. You cannot simply pick the verses of Scripture you like and then discard the ones that don't fit you. You cannot treat salvation like Pandora radio—just keep pressing the X button until you hear only the messages you like.

The message that Jesus preached cannot be custom fit to gel with your present philosophies and ideologies. Everyone must go to the cross in order to reach heaven. There simply is no other way. The cross is the portal to anything and everything Jesus. We cannot have the Savior without the broken body or the spilled blood. And not only must we accept His brokenness, but we must be partakers of the cross.

> *That I may know him, and the power of his resurrection, and the fellowship of his sufferings, being made conformable unto his death* (Philippians 3:10).

My Kingdom, His Kingdom

When we come to the Lord, death should occur in that "I-life" we are so fond of. This, however, is totally against every part of our carnal nature. We are wired for personal survival. Some have an easier time sacrificing their physical lives for a good cause than surrendering their personal beliefs.

What I mean is, the same man who will run inside a burning building to save a life may never surrender iLife to Jesus. We are geared toward guarding our own personal kingdom, of which we are the king.

For instance, when Alexander the Great would conquer a foreign land, the first thing that had to happen was the present king must give up his throne and hand it to Alexander, the new king. There can never be a scenario where the fallen king retains his throne. No country could declare allegiance to Rome without first removing their present king, and this was usually by the death of that king.

When we enter the kingdom of God, we must first remove the king of our own kingdom, and that happens at the cross. Every king must die in order to allow Jesus Christ to rule as our new and present King. Many want to call Jesus their King yet retain their own authority and dominion over their personal lives. This cannot be possible. Total surrender literally means . . . death to self.

I like to adopt the apostle Paul's thoughts on this and personally declare of myself: "I am free from the body of sin and the bonds of Satan, and now my Lord and my Master is Jesus Christ of Whom I am now a prisoner to His kingdom. I am in the bonds of His gospel; I am a servant and a slave to His way of thinking."

So my mind is not free to think as it used to. We have to denounce everything in the realm of iDesire and iWant. We need learn to pray, "Thy kingdom come." More than simply speaking the words of the Lord's Prayer, when we pray those words, we are invoking the constant presence of the cross in our daily lives. Paul said:

> *[I assure you] by the pride which I have in you in [your fellowship and union with] Christ Jesus our Lord, that I die daily [I face*

death every day and die to self] (I Corinthians 15:31, AMP).

When Paul prayed the Lord's Prayer, he was praying, "Let this king die and become subject to the new order. I surrender to the new King." If we want the benefits of the kingdom of God, we must go to the cross and die. We must partake in His death that we may also partake in the Resurrection (Romans 6:5; Philippians 3:10).

When Jesus questioned His disciples, "Will ye also go away?" (John 6:67), He was in essence asking them, "Will you punch the dislike button and walk away?" Their answer was profound and incredibly insightful to our response to the message of the cross: "Lord, to whom shall we go? thou hast the words of eternal life." Let that be the prayer of each of us. Let that answer become so ingrained into our very being that it becomes not only our words but actually how we feel.

Your Best Life Now vs. the Doctrine of Suffering

The best-selling book by Joel Osteen, *Your Best Life Now*, is in reality the best-selling concept to a world that is intoxicated with self. This message, however, was not the message of Christ, nor was it the message of the New Testament church. Now, do not get me wrong; there is no question that I am truly living my best life now since I surrendered myself to this precious gospel. Nevertheless, any teaching that focuses solely on your best life now rather than your best life in eternity will cease to teach about judgment, hell, and self-denial and will ultimately remove any teaching regarding the sacrifice it takes to get to heaven. The doctrine of suffering is certainly not how any minister would market his church to attract new converts . . . unless he was Jesus, of course.

Jesus spoke about suffering often. You must die to live (Matthew 10:39), and "I will shew him how great things he must suffer for my name's sake" (Acts 9:16). Jesus asked people to suffer emotionally by walking away from their families (Mark 10:29-30). Jesus told them to suffer the loss of their income and earthly possessions in order to be His disciples (Mark 10:21).

This teaching can be hard for anyone to take. I will be honest with you, when we want folks to visit our church, we lure them with "feel good" emotions with good food, dramatic presentations, the kids' choir, or a message of healing, hope, and deliverance. You will not likely see a church flyer saying something like:

> *Come to First Church of Anytown, where you can give all your money to the poor, leave your loved ones behind, resign your career, and follow after Jesus and where you will most likely be killed for that decision.*

Granted, Jesus did lure them in with a free potluck fish-and-chips dinner, but then He wasted no time in calling out everyone in the crowd for his or her selfish and carnal motives. The teaching of the cross is offensive but necessary.

The Witness Protection Program

So what in these few men enabled them not to be offended at these words? Eventually they did give up everything for Jesus. They truly did surrender all. It is almost comical to see folks squirm when we begin to teach on tithing. But what if you were asked to live your ministry within the confines of a Roman jail? What then? Others have issues with the modest lifestyle that is taught in the Word of God. They say, "I do not believe God cares about what we wear." (Notice the use of the "I" in the statement, and see I Timothy 2:9.) Yet these men were asked to die as martyrs for their dedication to the name of Jesus. Some feel it's a "hard" teaching when the pastor encourages us to stop watching ungodly movies and abstain from secular music or to show up for church services more than once per week. Others shun the thought of being an usher or a hostess at the church as it may require too much of a commitment. But these men were asked to be fed to lions and preach the gospel to a society until they were stoned to death.

Jesus asks us to spend more time with Him than we do on anything else, yet the lives of most of us would not in any way testify of our love for Him. Rather, we spend hours on Facebook, video games, the computer, and television with little to no time working in ministry or serving the kingdom. The preacher calls for repentance or, should I say, begins to preach the doctrine of the cross, and the crowd thins to a mere handful of believers.

So what made these men so able to commit to this doctrine of suffering and death to self? What made them so "super-spiritual"? How can we receive the Word of God with gladness, no matter what chapter and verse we are on? Was it that they witnessed miracles? Maybe. Was it the preaching of Jesus in the hills of Judea? Possibly some. Maybe it was the hope of salvation and eternal life? Most likely all of the above. But wasn't this really seen and heard by all, even the ones who eventually walked away?

Let us consider John, the one whom they called the beloved of Christ. These two had a special relationship. John was not just one of the twelve original disciples but one of the inner circle. When Jesus proclaimed that one would betray Him, while all the others were asking, "Is it I?" John was the one who leaned upon the bosom of Jesus and asked, "Who is it, Lord?" He knew it wasn't going to be him. Of all those who had a close relationship with Jesus, this young, impressionable, soft-spoken gentleman and friend is the one I want to draw your attention to.

You see, Jesus not only taught us about suffering, He lived it . . . even to the death of the cross. This was the darkest hour of Jesus' life. Much study and many scholars have exhausted themselves writing about the details of the agony experienced by our Savior during the time of the cross. While I give honor to those who have attempted to give us understanding, I believe there really is no way possible to comprehend the horror of Calvary. To begin to describe the torture, the scourging, the defilement of body and character, and the humiliation of the cruelest manner would be futile for our complete comprehension. We know that death by crucifixion is bloody. Try, if you will, to imagine the torture, the screams, the anguish, and the suffering that occurred at Calvary. For those who actually witnessed this horrific event, it must have been catastrophic.

Here, at the foot of the cross, we find Jesus' trusted friend, John the beloved. John was not hiding with the other disciples; he would stay with His master until the very end. But wouldn't we expect that of John?

John was a witness. I want to key in on that for a moment. John was an eyewitness to this atrocity. John saw the torn flesh. He could see the exposed rib bones of his loving Lord. He viewed the blood dripping from the crown of thorns, down the broken vessels on His face, and across the naked body. The cross, for John, was not a concept; it was real. This wasn't something that John heard about Easter Sunday at his local church or read in some ancient book.

John heard the hammer clang against the nine-inch nails. He could hear the gasping and the screaming of Jesus. John heard every moan and every whisper. "Here is the Word made flesh, God incarnate, my friend, my Savior, withering away to nothing." Again, it is unimaginable for us really to know what this was like for all who saw it. In the midst of this horrific event, John's world must have come to a complete standstill; time must have frozen when John heard the voice of the Lamb of God speak his name while suspended between heaven and earth.

While the blood flowed from His wounds, Jesus called to John, "Behold thy mother!" (John 19:27). Jesus cried out to John from the cross. Even in the last moments of agony, the Master was concerned about the well-being of His friend. I cannot know nor begin to understand what John must have felt to witness this event, but when I read the First Epistle of John 1:1, I am greatly moved by the words John expressed.

When he declared to a people who were beginning to fall into the belief that Jesus was not actually a man who suffered and literally died, John's desperate plea was:

> *That which was from the beginning, which we have heard, which we have seen with our eyes, which we have looked upon, and our hands have handled, of the Word of life* (I John 1:1).

I cannot help but believe that as John penned these words, he remembered the day he witnessed the cross. It was like John was saying, "I saw Him. You were not there, but I was. You don't know what I have seen. You don't know how it felt when I heard Jesus call to me from the cross. Where else will I go, to whom will I turn now? No one else. Once you've been to the cross, there simply is no other place to go."

You see, John was in the Witness Protection Program. His experience (his witness) at Calvary caused him to surrender his life totally to Jesus. Neither the miracles that he witnessed nor even the wonders caused these men to die to life and turn completely to Him. It certainly wasn't thoughts of "your best life now" or praying the prayer of Jabez. It wasn't another Beth Moore book on victorious Christian living that enabled John to face death. It was Calvary!

After you have been to Calvary, there is no turning back. Peter wrote these words after Calvary: "For even hereunto were ye called: because Christ also suffered for us, leaving us an example, that ye should follow his steps" (I Peter 2:21). When you are a witness of the cross, you too enter the Witness Protection Program. In other words, you're sold out to this. There is no other option for you. Once you hear the call from Calvary, there simply is no turning back.

The Cross Is Personal

I believe this is a truth: I cannot save anyone, I cannot convince anyone to die to self, I cannot persuade anyone with fair words or good speeches, but if I can get you to the cross . . . if I can lead you to Calvary, friend, you will hear from God. He will call your name, and you will surrender your kingdom. You will say the words of the apostles, "There is nowhere else for me to go. To whom shall we go? For You, dear Lord, hold the keys to eternal life."

> *Whoever abides in Him does not sin. Whoever sins has neither seen Him nor known Him* (I John 3:6, NKJV).

If you struggle with old desires and continue to sin, something is missing from your experience with God. John's expression here may seem hard, but think about what John saw at Cavalry. Consider, if you will, his perspective for a moment. "If you continue to sin, you must not have seen what I have seen; you must not have known Jesus like I have." If you can hear Jesus call your name from Calvary, you will no longer fight that old man. The former king of that old kingdom will be dead.

There is a level of going beyond knowing about the cross and becoming a partaker of it. When you have been to the cross, you will have eaten the flesh and drunk the blood. The cross will become a part of your innermost being. The Lamb of God will not be a mere story in a book, but He will be in you. The Lamb of God will give you nourishment and substance. (We will discuss this more in a later chapter.)

For John, the cross was intensely personal. Yet because the cross is not a past event but an ever-present reality for everyone, the cross can be personal for you as well.

I was an atheist who was led to the foot of the cross. I was a sinner of sinners. I was lost without a hope at all in this world. I was a man who was crushed by guilt and shame. My past mistakes were ever before me. Everything I had done in my past was forging my future. I was a failure, and I was in desperate need of forgiveness from my children, my wife, my friends, and my family. At the lowest part of my life, I can honestly say, God called me to the cross.

How do I know it was the cross? Because I felt the presence of a God I did not even believe existed. I began to feel the weight of my sins, as if they were being drawn out of me. Sins that I had not even acknowledged or even known were suddenly exposed. My failures were present, and my past was a weight I could not bear. My heart began to break, and my eyes filled with tears. I was broken.

Friend, let me tell you, this is what happens when you get to the cross. This is the cross present and relevant in your life. At the foot of Calvary, you feel the presence of a dying Savior; you acknowledge your sins, guilt, and shame; and then, just like for John, it happens. Jesus calls out to you from the depths of your despair. You hear Him say to you, "Behold, My son, I will provide you a comforter for your brokenness."

Jesus began speaking to me . . . *me*, that's right. Jesus spoke to me from the cross. He spoke things to me that only I knew about myself. He told me, "I forgive you." I remember it so vividly. I felt Him say to my brokenness, "I forgive you," and somehow I knew what it cost Him to take away my sin, lift my guilt, and remove my shame.

Jesus took my place on the cross. My trip to Calvary acknowledged that He was on my cross. The heaviness of guilt lifted off me. At the cross I let go of my life. I surrendered my broken life to Him. The more I surrendered to Him, the lighter the burden became. At the cross I saw Him as King of my life. There I died to myself.

Friend, when you hear God call your name from Calvary, there simply is no turning back. I will forever hold fast to the foot of that old rugged tree. At the cross God called me, saved me, delivered me, and forgave me. I will never forget the day of the cross.

I understand how Paul could say, "I die to myself daily," because every time I relive those wonderful moments of the cross, I die all over again, I surrender all over again. I try to live my life under the shadow of my personal Calvary. This event happened to me years before I wrote this book, yet it is not an event in my past. The cross experience for me is forever present and relevant. It must be. This keeps my old man dead and my new man alive. More details of my personal experience can be found in *I Was An Atheist: But God* by the same author.

Carnal Kings Must Die

When I speak about how you must die to yourself at the cross, some may initially think that this would be a hard thing to do. Most of us are very fond of ourselves. We want to protect ourselves. If we give up our kingdom, we may feel that we have lost the battle to survive. This is what happens to folks when they try to enter the kingdom of God without going to the cross. They neglect to see the true benefit of killing that old man of our carnal nature and surrendering to the new King. They do not have the revelation that their king (themselves) is actually their deadliest enemy.

This is like when Israel wanted a king. They asked Samuel, "Now make us a king to judge us like all the nations" (I Samuel 8:5b). They were asking to be led by a king as the other "worldly" kings. God then described what a carnally minded king would be like. This description is exactly what we are like as we rule our own kingdom. See if this description resembles your carnal nature as you rule your kingdom:

> *And he said, This will be the manner of the king that shall reign over you: He will take your sons, and appoint them for himself, for his chariots, and to be his horsemen; and some shall run before his chariots. And he will appoint him captains over thousands, and captains over fifties; and will set them to ear his ground, and to reap his harvest, and to make his instruments of war, and instruments of his chariots. And he will take your daughters to be confectionaries, and to be cooks, and to be bakers. And he will take your fields, and your vineyards, and your oliveyards, even the best of them, and give them to his servants. And he will take the tenth of your seed, and of your vineyards, and give to his officers, and to his servants. And he will take your menservants, and your maidservants, and your goodliest young men, and your asses, and put them to his work. He will take the tenth of*

your sheep: and ye shall be his servants (I Samuel 8:11-17).

This describes a king who will consume everything for himself. Intoxicated with selfishness, he will feed himself with lust and greed, live for the now, and lay up nothing for the future. Lust for flesh, love of money, and hunger for power will cause him to destroy his own family, burn up his own fields, and ultimately destroy himself. God describes this type of man as a dictator and not a leader.

At the cross, we see ourselves through the eyes of God. There I realized who the enemy truly was, and it was at the cross I realized what had to happen in order to save myself. . . . I had to die.

Consider this; the only way God's chosen king, David, could take the throne of Israel was if Saul died. We see this happening in I Samuel 31:4 when Saul, knowing that he had lost the battle, fell upon his own sword and died. Like Saul, we have to give ourselves willingly so that God's King can rule our kingdom. The contrast between Saul's method of rule and David's is vast. Saul was a man who fed his own heart; David was a man after God's heart. David was not perfect, but if you look at the dynasty of King David, you will see that our new King, Jesus, is part of the kingship of David, the man who replaced Saul (II Samuel 7:13-16; Isaiah 9:7).

I believe it was Charles Spurgeon who prayed, "Lord, I pray that my carnal man receive a fatal blow by the sword of the Spirit, that is the Word of God, that my spiritual man may live." At the cross, we have no problem laying on the sword and taking a fatal blow to the flesh. This death at Calvary is not burdensome, hard, or even difficult. This death becomes a moment of triumph and victory in our lives. We never mourn the death of our king Saul; we rejoice that Jesus, who won our victory, reigns in our lives. For He is truly the

Servant King. Jesus will never take advantage of us. In His kingdom, we will never be used and abused. Jesus will never abuse His power to serve Himself. We understand what David wrote in Psalm 23.

> *The LORD is my shepherd; I shall not want. He maketh me to lie down in green pastures: he leadeth me beside the still waters. He restoreth my soul: he leadeth me in the paths of righteousness for his name's sake. Yea, though I walk through the valley of the shadow of death, I will fear no evil: for thou art with me; thy rod and thy staff they comfort me. Thou preparest a table before me in the presence of mine enemies: thou anointest my head with oil; my cup runneth over. Surely goodness and mercy shall follow me all the days of my life: and I will dwell in the house of the LORD for ever.*

A Study of the Cross

Concerning our new lives with Christ, the apostles always lead us back to two truths on which we should base our lives: No pain compares to the glory that is set before us, and no sacrifice compares to that of Calvary. Because of the great significance the cross has on our Christian existence, it is vital that we learn as much as possible about it. This book is dedicated to the importance of our understanding the value of the cross in our lives. I believe that we can and will be overcomers by the power of the cross.

This book is not meant to be the beginning and the ending of all that Calvary means to us as Christians. It is, however, the breaking away of the surface that will hopefully inspire us all to dig deeper into God's Word for more understanding and revelation. Join me as we enter into the *Crux of the Matter: A Study of the Cross*.

Chapter Two

Victory in Revelation

Having wiped out the handwriting of requirements that was against us, which was contrary to us. And He has taken it out of the way, having nailed it to his cross. Having disarmed principalities and powers, He made a public spectacle of them, triumphing over them in it (Colossians 2:14-15, NKJV).

As we begin our study of the cross, I feel that a foundation should be established, groundwork, if you will, that we will use to build upon as we journey through the many aspects of the cross. This chapter will serve as that foundation. It is paramount that we understand more was accomplished at Calvary than just the forgiveness of sins. I do not intend to minimize the importance of that truth but rather to maximize the importance of all the other truths about the cross.

I believe that if we, the church, could ever begin to comprehend the total sum of all that the cross did for us, we would live greater and abundant lives. In other words, if you knew what God did for you at the cross, the devil would not have access to your life as he may today. I see many Christians who struggle with a lack of joy and peace and are crippled with fear, anxiety, and doubt. Many born-again believers struggle with shame over past and present failures and oftentimes operate under a handicap in the gifts of the Spirit. It is time to live in the power that was afforded to us at Calvary and serve the devil an eviction notice. He has been trespassing on the real estate taken from him at the cross.

We Are All Born Sinners

We are all born sinners. Great revelation, right? I assume that if you are reading this book, you may already know this truth. But allow me to set the stage, if you will. It all happened at the Fall in the Garden of Eden. Adam and Eve lived in blissful communion with God and each other. There, the devil lied to Eve and convinced her that it was "good" to become like God.

> *Then the serpent said to the woman, "You will not surely die. For God knows that in the day you eat of it your eyes will be opened, and you will be like God, knowing good and evil"* (Genesis 3:4-5, NKJV).

The foundation of the devil's kingdom was established upon one simple question: can there be more than one God? This is the question Lucifer asked himself, which in turn caused him to be cast out of heaven.

> *"How you are fallen from heaven, O Lucifer, son of the morning! How you are cut down to the ground, You who weakened the nations! For you have said in your heart: 'I will ascend into heaven, I will exalt my throne above the stars of God; I will also sit on the mount of the congregation on the farthest sides of the north; I will ascend above the heights of the*

*clouds, **I will be like the Most High**' "* (Isaiah 14:12-14, NKJV, emphasis mine).

Notice Lucifer did not want to be above God but rather to become "like" God. That was the question that got him kicked out of heaven, and that was the lie told Eve. Remember this: when we stand and declare that there is only one God, it shakes the devil's kingdom. The Bible tells us that the devil trembles in fear at the knowledge that there is only one God. ("Thou believest that there is one God; thou doest well: the devils also believe, and tremble" [James 2:19].) Any doctrine that suggests there is more than one God is birthed from the heart of Satan. Every time we gather together and lift our hands to heaven and declare that Jesus is the only One worthy of praise . . . the devils tremble.

Eve, unfortunately, took the bait. She ate from the tree and then Adam followed. This was the original sin. The first Adam did not maintain his righteous state. Adam and Eve became defiled. They both experienced a spiritual death. This sin was irreversible. At this moment, there was no option of repentance. There was no way to have this sin erased. I am so thankful to be living in the dispensation of grace, when we can now run to the cross and allow the blood of Jesus to cleanse us from all unrighteousness.

For Adam and Eve this simply was not an option; this sin (corruption) affected both their physical DNA and the spiritual DNA. Eve then conceived and bore a son. This child was created by the corrupted DNA of his fallen mother and father. Adam was created in the image and likeness of God (Genesis 5:1); however, Adam's son was created in the image and likeness of Adam (Genesis 5:3), the fallen man. Every child that is born has been born with an infected bloodline. That which is born of this fallen, sinful nature is the product of that fallen state (John 3:6). Paul said it like this:

> *Therefore, just as sin entered the world through one man, and death through sin, in this way death spread to all men, because all sinned* (Romans 5:12, HCSB).

We will explore this more in detail in a later chapter, but for now, it's important to understand that when we are born, we are sinners. Our actions are not what cause us to become sinners but rather our spiritual state. We are all born lost and in need of salvation.

The Documents against Us

> *Having cancelled and blotted out and wiped away the handwriting of the note (bond) with its legal decrees and demands which was in force and stood against us (hostile to us). This [note with its regulations, decrees, and demands] He set aside and cleared completely out of our way by nailing it to [His] cross. [God] disarmed the principalities and powers that were ranged against us and made a bold display and public example of them, in triumphing over them in Him and in it [the cross]* (Colossians 2:14-15, AMP).

When we are born, we are already violating the holy ordinances of God. We are lawbreakers and are trespassing the righteous laws of a holy God. To further complicate our fallen state, add all of the actual sins that we commit. We bear not just the sinful nature of our fallen ancestor Adam but every sin that we have committed personally. Every thought, every deed, every lie . . . everything we have ever done. It may be hard to wrap our minds around; it is not the simple fact that we have committed certain sins. The truth is that all we have ever done is sin. Every day we live outside the kingdom of God, we are sinning. Every day we live without giving praise to the one true and living God, we are sinning. If we do anything at all without giving God thought or acknowledgment, we are sinning.

Some people ask, "If I live a good life and never lie, cheat, or steal, do I still need to believe in Jesus to be saved?" The short answer is found in John 3.

> *Jesus answered, "Most assuredly, I say to you, unless one is born of water and the Spirit, he cannot enter the kingdom of God. That which is born of the flesh is flesh, and that which is born of the Spirit is spirit"* (John 3:5-6, NKJV).

The process of being born again begins at Calvary. The term "flesh" here is from the Greek word *sarx*, meaning (by implication) our human nature (with its frailties [physically or morally] and passions). This describes our carnal-mindedness or sinful nature. Everything we do while in the state of unrighteousness (or flesh) is unrighteous (flesh). In order to break free from this sinful state, we must be born again of the water and the Spirit, born of the Spirit of God. (See Acts 2:38; Colossians 2:8-12.)

So, because of our sinful condition, legal documents exist that are contrary to us. The term "handwritten" in Colossians 2:14 is from the Greek word *cheirographon*, meaning something handwritten, i.e. a manuscript (specifically, **a legal document or bond**). These documents contain our sins before God. They are the judgments against us, and they are valid. These documents do not contain lies from our adversary but rather they are truths about us, and they are hostile to us.

I find it interesting that Paul used the word "handwritten," indicating something was done personally, with precise intent. Someone took the time to write every sin we ever committed. These are the documents that will be used at our time of judgment. When we stand before God, these documents will be laid out beside the law of God, and we will be judged according to these legal documents. What we see Paul describing here is what figuratively happened when Jesus went to the cross. Jesus took our personal offenses, these legally binding decrees, and He nailed them to the cross.

This is vitally important for us, to understand the power of the cross and the victory that we experience because of the cross. Let this sink into your spirit for a moment; everything that Jesus took to the cross was left at the cross. Let me restate this again: everything that was nailed to the cross was swallowed up into a spiritual vortex. Whatever Jesus took there was broken. It was removed. These legal documents became null and void at the cross.

Consider how our justice system works. When someone is accused of a horrible crime, the prosecuting attorney must provide hard evidence against the accused. This hard evidence could be a number of things. It could be a DNA sample from the scene of the crime, fingerprints on the weapon, or best yet, an eyewitness. This hard evidence is presented at the courtroom on the day of the trial. Without these documents of proof, the prosecuting attorney simply has no case at all. The prosecutor becomes powerless to make any accusations at all. The accused, whether he is guilty or innocent, will simply walk free.

This is what Paul explained to us in Colossians 2. The accused is you or I, the prosecuting attorney is none other than the devil himself, and the Judge is God. The Bible refers to the devil as our accuser (Revelation 12:10). This term refers to a legal accuser in an assembly of law.

Jesus, who is our legal defense attorney and is called our "advocate" (I John 2:1), has stripped (disarmed) the devil by taking all of his hard evidence against you and me and nailing it to His cross. The devil has lost all power to execute any further advances against us.

> *He set aside and cleared completely out of our way by nailing it to [His] cross. [God] disarmed the principalities and powers that were ranged against us and made a bold display and public example of them, in triumphing over them in Him and in it [the cross]* (Colossians 2:14-15, AMP).

The Enemy Has No Case

The devil, your adversary, cannot accuse you any longer. Your record has been cleared, and your past has been erased. When you become convinced of this truth, the devil will never be able to haunt you with past mistakes. He should never be allowed to bring up old sins. There should never be an occasion when we allow him to remind us of things that were once written on those legal documents. Because of the cross, he has no more to say.

> *Forasmuch then as the children are partakers of flesh and blood, he also himself likewise took part of the same; that through death he might destroy him that had the power of death, that is, the devil* (Hebrews 2:14).

Did you get that? He said that because we are in flesh, God took on the nature of humanity. And by going through death (that is to say, the cross), Jesus destroyed the devil. The word "destroy" is defined by the Strong's NT:2673 *katargeo* (kat-arg-eh'-o); to (render) entirely (useless), abolish, cease, destroy, do away, to (make) of no effect, fail, bring (come) to nought, put (down), vanish away, make void.

> *Since, therefore, [these His] children share in flesh and blood [in the physical nature of human beings], He [Himself] in a similar manner partook of the same [nature], that by [going through] death He might bring to nought and make of no effect him who had the power of death—that is, the devil* (Hebrews 2:14, AMP).

All the devil can do to us is accuse us, for he is the accuser of the brethren. And until the cross he had a very good case against us. But now that Jesus took those documents and nailed them to His cross, the devil has been rendered totally useless.

The next verse explains how this affects us. "And deliver them who through fear of death were all their lifetime subject to bondage" (Hebrews 2:15). The devil has nothing else to use as hard evidence; therefore, as a prosecuting attorney, he has lost his power. His case against you has been rendered totally null and void.

What incredible victory we have! We have been released from this haunting fear of death. Read it in the Amplified Version for greater emphasis.

> *And also that He might deliver and completely set free all those who through the [haunting] fear of death were held in bondage throughout the whole course of their lives* (Hebrews 2:15, AMP).

The Lord Rebuke You, Satan!

The devil knows that he has no power to accuse you. He knows that there is no more hard evidence that he can use to get a conviction. But he is counting on your not knowing this truth. As long as you don't realize this, he has access to torment your mind. This is the reason we are stricken with fear. We are confused about life and the direction God wants us to take. The enemy will make you feel that you are not worthy of God's calling in your life. You will never be able to operate in the gifts of the Spirit as long as you are still feeling like a sinner who is unclean and unforgiven. I want you to know this: God has an anointing for you and a ministry for you to step into. Your past sins were nailed to the tree and swallowed up in victory. You have rights that the devil will never understand, nor will he ever have access to those rights.

The Old Testament is our servant leader (schoolmaster) that brings us to Christ. As we look into the pages of the law and the prophets, we will gain much understanding of what the cross has done for us. The prophet Zechariah had much to say about the Messiah. Look at Zechariah 3:1-5 to see how he described the day when God will shut the mouth of our accuser.

> *Then he showed me Joshua the high priest standing before the Angel of the LORD, and Satan standing at his right hand to oppose him* (Zechariah 3:1, NKJV).

Zechariah saw in this vision the current high priest of Israel, Joshua. There is no doubt Zechariah knew Joshua and had dealings with him. Zechariah must have seen him frequently as Joshua carried out his priestly duties. But here, in Zechariah's vision, Joshua was being accused as a common criminal. Satan stood at Joshua's right hand. This would be symbolic of Satan having power or authority over him. So the picture that is being described here is that Joshua, the high priest of Israel stood as a prisoner of Satan. Joshua was violently accused of sins. Matthew Henry states:

> Joshua is accused as a criminal, but is justified. 1. A violent opposition is made to him. Satan stands at his right hand to resist him to be a Satan to him, a law-adversary. He stands at his right hand, as the prosecutor, or witness, at the right hand of the prisoner. Note, The devil is the accuser of the brethren, that accuses them before God day and night, Rev 12:10. Some think the chief priest was accused for the sin of many of the inferior priests, in marrying strange wives, which they were much guilty of after their return out of captivity, Ezra 9:1, 2; Neh 13:28. When God is about to reestablish the priesthood Satan objects the sins that were found among the priests, as rendering them unworthy the honour designed them. It is by our own folly that we give Satan advantage against us and furnish him with matter for reproach and accusation; and if any thing be amiss, especially with the priests, Satan will be sure to aggravate it and make the worst of it. He stood to resist him, that is, to oppose the service he was doing for the public good. He stood at his right hand, the hand of action, to discourage him, and raise difficulties in his way. Note, When we stand before God to minister to him, or stand up for God to serve his interests, we

> must expect to meet with all the resistance that Satan's subtlety and malice can give us. Let us then resist him that resists us and he shall flee from us.[2]

And this is how the Lord responded to Satan:

> *And the LORD said to Satan, "The LORD rebuke you, Satan! The LORD who has chosen Jerusalem rebuke you! Is this not a brand plucked from the fire?" [I have tried him in the fire for sins but I have not destroyed him. . . . I have taken him from the fire.] Now Joshua was clothed with filthy garments, and was standing before the Angel* (Zechariah 3:2-3, NKJV).

Zechariah now saw that Joshua was disqualified to be the intercessor for Israel. For truly, there is no man worthy to stand in this office. This is the reality of the vision set before Zechariah. What a tragedy! Who will be able to stand and to intercede for lost humanity? Who will ever be able to be a high priest and enter into the presence of a holy God on behalf of fallen man?

Joshua's true sins were exposed through his filthy garments. The high priest's holiness was represented through his outward display of priestly robes. His "pure" garments, worn for all men to see, signified that Joshua was holy and sanctified for the work in the Temple. But Zechariah could see the

---

[2]*Matthew Henry's Commentary on the Whole Bible*, PC Study Bible Formatted Electronic Database. Copyright © 2006 by Biblesoft, Inc. All rights reserved.

holy man as God sees us all: "But we are all like an unclean thing, and all our righteousnesses are like filthy rags" (Isaiah 64:6, NKJV). Through the eyes of God, we are unrighteous and filthy. Here we stand as Satan's prisoner of sin.

Satan stood and declared Joshua's sin before God. "This man is disqualified to serve; there is no man who can intercede for the sinners." But then we see the intent of this vision. It was not for Zechariah to see the hidden sins of his high priest but rather to see the redemptive plan of God through the cross of Jesus Christ.

The Lord stood and rebuked Satan, declaring to him, "I have plucked him (Joshua) out of the fire." The Lord is none other than Jesus Christ, our righteous Judge. With nail-scarred hands, Jesus rebukes Satan. "Have I not saved him from judgment? Did I not take his legal charges and all the evidence against him to My cross?" Jesus rebukes him and reminds him that he has been made utterly powerless.

> *Then [the Lord] He answered and spoke to those who stood before Him, saying, "Take away the filthy garments from him." And to him He said, "See, I have removed your iniquity from you, and I will clothe you with rich robes." And I said, "Let them put a clean turban on his head"* (Zechariah 3:4-5, NKJV).

Now, here is the best part. You have to visualize what just happened here to comprehend it fully. Remember, you have a filthy prisoner who is guilty as charged. His clothes are the evidence that the charges against him are true. You have standing at his right hand, in total authority over him, the law accuser viciously attacking him and declaring his sins before God. The prisoner is subject to Satan. I visualize Joshua kneeling and Satan towering over him, holding the chains that bind the prisoner. Watch this: right in front of the accuser, the Lord took away his filthy garments and clothed him with a cloak of righteousness.

> *I will greatly rejoice in the LORD, my soul shall be joyful in my God;* ***for he hath clothed me with the garments of salvation, he hath covered me with the robe of righteousness****, as a bridegroom decketh himself with ornaments, and as a bride adorneth herself with her jewels* (Isaiah 61:10, emphasis mine).

After Jesus clothed Joshua in righteousness, He then told the bystanders to put a clean turban upon his head. If you read Exodus 28, you will discover the significance of the clothes and especially the turban. The robes and turban are worn so that the high priest can be accepted before the Lord, so that the sacrifice for the iniquity of the people can be accepted. The turban represents headship and total authority. The new turban gave authority back to the man of God. The office of high priest had been restored.

So here we see God taking the chains off the accused and placing them on the accuser. Satan has become the prisoner, and we have become the lawaccuser. "Resist the devil, and he will flee from you" (James 4:7). We now can resist or oppose him the same way he used to oppose us, and we have authority over him. We received this power by the cross.

> *For the accuser of our brethren is cast down, which accused them before our God day and night. And they overcame him by the blood of the Lamb, and by the word of their testimony; and they loved not their lives unto the death* (Revelation 12:10b-11).

Hast Thou Not Known?

> *All heaven is interested in the cross of Christ, all hell is terribly afraid of it, while men are the only beings who more or less ignore its meaning* (Oswald Chambers).

John told us the reason that Jesus came was to defeat the enemy. "The reason the Son of God was made manifest (visible) was to undo (destroy, loosen, and dissolve) the works the devil [has done]" (I John 3:8b, AMP). Everything that the devil has done has been dissolved. John reiterated this point to remind the saints of God that our relationship with the devil has changed since the cross. We are no longer under the rule of Satan (John 8:34). We are no longer sinners; therefore, we should not serve sin (I John 3:3-10). We should never forget what the Lord has freed us from, that we not fall prey to the snare of the enemy.

We have been given some great and precious promises in the Word of God. Isaiah prophesied about a church that was purchased by the blood of Christ at Calvary when he stated: " 'No weapon forged against you will prevail, and you will refute every tongue that accuses you. This is the heritage of the servants of the LORD, and this is their vindication from me,' declares the LORD" (Isaiah 54:17, NIV). There is no weapon that the blacksmith can forge that will be greater than the blood of Jesus. You will never be in a position where the devil can overtake you. Remember, his weapons are the documents against you that have been nailed to the cross.

In addition to the weapons forged by the enemy, every accusation will be silenced. Notice how the power is given to you: "and ***you will*** refute every tongue." The Lord, through His victory, has given us power to refute the accusations against us. The word "accuses" here refers to a legal verdict that is pronounced judicially against you, specifically in a criminal court. Our power to ward off every dart the devil can throw at us and every accusation that he speak against us is our "heritage" as saints of God. This is part of our inheritance granted to us from the first-born from the dead, the last Adam (Colossians 1:13-22).

We have been given authority over the enemy.

> *My sheep hear my voice, and I know them, and they follow me: and I give unto them eternal life; and they shall never perish, neither shall any man pluck them out of my hand. My Father, which gave them me, is greater than all; and no man is able to pluck them out of my Father's hand* (John 10:27-29).

Jesus manifested Himself on earth so that He could disarm the devil. He has gone through the torture of the cross in order to free us from the hand of Satan. With those same nail-scarred hands He holds us, preserves us, and keeps us from all harm whatsoever. Do you think, after all that the Lord has endured to save us, that He would allow a fallen angel to "pluck" you out of those hands? I think not!

> *Hast thou not known? hast thou not heard, that the everlasting God, the LORD, the Creator of the ends of the earth, fainteth not, neither is weary? there is no searching of his understanding. He giveth power to the faint; and to them that have no might he increaseth strength. Even the youths shall faint and be weary, and the young men shall utterly fall: but they that wait upon the LORD shall renew their strength; they shall mount up with wings*

> *as eagles; they shall run, and not be weary; and they shall walk, and not faint* (Isaiah 40:28-31).

Not only has He given us power to resist the devil, but Jesus has given us power to advance upon the devil. We must understand that in order truly to live the abundant life that God has willed for us, we must see the devil's kingdom through the eyes of a victorious church. Jesus has established His church by the death, burial, and resurrection.

> *And I say also unto thee, That thou art Peter, and upon this rock I will build my church;* ***and the gates of hell shall not prevail against it****. . . . and whatsoever thou shalt bind on earth shall be bound in heaven: and whatsoever thou shalt loose on earth shall be loosed in heaven* (Matthew 16:18-19, emphasis mine).

The gates of hell mean the devil and his kingdom. This charge is not supposed to put the church in a defensive mode but rather in an offensive mode. This does not give us a picture of a saint of God who is merely standing his ground or simply maintaining position. This, however, does give the vision of an army who has just realized that their archenemy has been rendered defenseless, and they are now moving in for the final, victorious attack.

Think of it this way: this war has raged for centuries. The enemy has ravaged us, beaten us down, mercilessly slaughtered our children, raped our women, and demoralized our men. We are on the front lines, and the battle with the enemy rages on and on. We have no real weapons to defend ourselves; we are literally at the mercy of this tyrant the devil. Just when we think that enemy is going to overtake us . . . we see Him. A man walks toward us, coming from the capital city of the enemy's territory. His clothes are stained with blood. It is apparent that he has been in a great battle of His own. Although He has been in battle, we see Him marching majestically, stately if you will, throwing back His head in conquest. He is not fatigued whatsoever, and His stature is that of some great champion.

He then calls out to us (lost humanity), "It is I, who speaks in righteousness, mighty to save." It is the warrior of God, heaven's Savior, the King of kings. We ask Him why His clothes are stained in blood. He answers, "I have trampled down your enemy. I had to go alone into the enemy's camp because there was no way anyone else could have defeated him. The blood you see on my clothes is the blood of your enemy. I have left him there, trodden down and defenseless. I have removed all of his artillery. There are no more weapons in his arsenal that can ever hurt you again. The enemy is there, beyond the gates of his kingdom, laying in defeat."

Then, the Lord hands us His sword and says: "Your enemy is defenseless; now go to finish him off. Not only him but tear down the gates of his kingdom, destroy the works of his hands. I give you power to bind every stronghold and to loose every imaginable reinforcement from heaven to completely dismember all that the enemy has done. Release his captives from chains, and claim every spoil of war for the glory of the kingdom of God."

> *Who is this who comes from Edom, with dyed garments from Bozrah, this One who is glorious in His apparel, traveling in the greatness of His strength?—"I who speak in righteousness, mighty to save." Why is Your apparel red, and Your garments like one who treads in the winepress? "I have trodden the winepress*

> *alone, and from the peoples no one was with Me. For I have trodden them in My anger, and trampled them in My fury; their blood is sprinkled upon My garments, and I have stained all My robes* (Isaiah 63:1-3, NKJV).

Every time you walk into a hospital, claim that place for the kingdom. Take spiritual dominion over every sickness and every disease. When you pray for your city, pray that every spirit of hell is bound and loose the Spirit of righteousness. Bind the spirit of perversion and loose the Spirit of holiness. Bind up the spirit of false doctrine and idol worship and loose the Spirit of truth and a Spirit of a hunger for truth. Dispatch from heaven the angels of Cornelius (Acts 10). Know this, you are the force that the devil does not have the power to overtake (Romans 16:20).

Fully Persuaded

In the Book of Romans, Paul was plain regarding this fact: if you walk in the flesh, you cannot partake in the victories of the cross. "There is therefore now no condemnation to them which are in Christ Jesus, who walk not after the flesh, but after the Spirit" (Romans 8:1).

Considering, then, that every born-again believer (Acts 2:38; 8:5-17; 19:1-6; 10) has power over the enemy, Paul closed the chapter thus:

> *What shall we then say to these things? If God be for us, who can be against us? He that spared not his own Son, but delivered him up for us all, how shall he not with him also freely give us all things? Who shall lay any thing to the charge of God's elect? It is God*

> *that justifieth. Who is he that condemneth? It is Christ that died, yea rather, that is risen again, who is even at the right hand of God, who also maketh intercession for us. Who shall separate us from the love of Christ? shall tribulation, or distress, or persecution, or famine, or nakedness, or peril, or sword? As it is written, For thy sake we are killed all the day long; we are accounted as sheep for the slaughter. Nay, in all these things we are more than conquerors through him that loved us. For I am persuaded, that neither death, nor life, nor angels, nor principalities, nor powers, nor things present, nor things to come, nor height, nor depth, nor any other creature, shall be able to separate us from the love of God, which is in Christ Jesus our Lord* (Romans 8:31-39).

The apostle Paul asked thought-provoking questions to some saints who may be allowing the devil to instill fear and guilt. He exclaimed, "There is no one to condemn you; there is no one who can lay any charge against you. You have been acquitted by God Himself, and you are held in His protective hand. Who or what shall pluck you from His hand? Who shall separate you from Christ? We should not fear any circumstance whatsoever—no danger, trial, hardship, fear itself, nor the thought of violent death." Paul declared we should not fear life or death, powers (rulers, spiritual or human), time (present or future events), or space (height nor depth). Think about that; all circumstances and time and space cover every dimension of man's finite thinking.

But just in case Paul missed something in the previous list, he covered it with "nor anything else in all creation."

What are you trying to say, Paul? We are victorious not only over the devil . . . but over every other thing as well. We have no external enemy at all. There is nothing that can get us; nothing can snatch us away. Nothing that our finite minds can dream up and nothing beyond what we can even imagine, there is simply nothing that can separate us from God's hand. When Isaiah said, "No weapon formed, no words spoken" will prosper against us, he was serious.

> *These things have I spoken unto you, being yet present with you. But the Comforter, which is the Holy Ghost, whom the Father will send in my name, he shall teach you all things, and bring all things to your remembrance, whatsoever I have said unto you. Peace I leave with you, my peace I give unto you: not as the world giveth, give I unto you.* ***Let not your heart be troubled, neither let it be afraid*** (John 14:25-27, emphasis mine).

The devil knows he is defeated. He knows you have the keys to his chains. He completely sees you as the powerful force that you are. All you have to do is "resist," just a little, and he must flee from you. He knows what liberty you have been given because of the cross. He knows you can cast him out by the power of the name and Spirit within you. He is well aware that you can destroy his gates in any city, any school, and any county . . . anywhere.

But here is the problem. As long as you are not aware of these truths, he can "deal wisely with you." The devil is good at one thing . . . being the devil. If we are ignorant, he is wise. "Be sober, be vigilant; because your adversary the devil, as a roaring lion, walketh about, seeking whom he may devour" (I Peter 5:8).

The devil is constantly searching for those whom he can devour. When we consider a lion's attack, we tend to think of some violent attack of ripping limbs and tearing flesh. The word "devour" that Peter used here means to slurp up, I suppose like someone eating a wiggly piece of Jello. So we see our adversary searching diligently for some dead piece of Jello that he can slurp up—certainly not the image of a lion trying to kill a fighting wildebeest. If you are alive in the Spirit, the devil will leave you alone, for he is not looking for a fight. But if you are dead in sin, you have become an easy meal for him.

> *And he said unto his people,* ***Behold, the people of the children of Israel are more and mightier than we:*** *come on, let us deal wisely with them; lest they multiply, and it come to pass, that, when there falleth out any war, they join also unto our enemies, and fight against us, and so get them up out of the land* (Exodus 1:9-10,emphasis mine).

The children of God had been given some great and precious promises, just as we have. They were told that God would make them a great and powerful nation. God told them that He would curse those who cursed them. No enemy would be able to prosper against them. They were living out the promises of God. The only problem was this: the enemy knew they were stronger and mightier, but Israel was clueless of this fact. They could have overthrown the Egyptian army and taken over the country. They could have become kings over Egypt, but instead they became slaves to those whom they could have conquered.

I believe we have allowed the enemy of our souls to have far too much freedom among the redeemed saints of

God. I know that none of us are perfect and that we all make mistakes, but we cannot allow the devil to weigh us down with guilt and shame. Conviction comes from God; it helps us to realize how we need to change and to conform into His image. Condemnation, on the other hand, is guilt placed on us by the devil. Satan has accused you too long. Take authority over him and cast him from your life. You have been set free by the blood of the Lamb.

I have heard some declare of themselves, "I am just a sinner." Friend, let me say that if you have been to Calvary and have repented of your sins, if you have been born again of the water and filled with the Holy Ghost, and if you live a holy life unto God (Acts 2:38-42), you may have been a sinner at one time, but you are no longer a child of wrath. You are no longer in chains of the devil. For . . .

> *you were washed, but you were sanctified, but you were justified in the name of the Lord Jesus and by the Spirit of our God* (I Corinthians 6:11b, NKJV).

My prayer is that we become fully persuaded of these truths. And may we walk in the power and the freedom that has been granted to us through the victory of the cross.

Chapter Three

Victory over Death, Hell, and the Grave!

But let me reveal to you a wonderful secret. We will not all die, but we will all be transformed! It will happen in a moment, in the blink of an eye, when the last trumpet is blown. For when the trumpet sounds, those who have died will be raised to live forever. And we who are living will also be transformed. For our dying bodies must be transformed into bodies that will never die; our mortal bodies must be transformed into immortal bodies. Then, when our dying bodies have been transformed into bodies that will never die, this Scripture will be fulfilled: "Death is swallowed up in victory. O death, where is your victory? O death, where is your sting?" For sin is the sting that results in death, and the law gives sin its power. But thank God! He gives us victory over sin and death through our Lord Jesus Christ (I Corinthians 15:51-57, NLT).

The greatest pall that hangs over mankind is the fear of death. In fact most things we fear find their source in the fear of death. The greatest fear of a mother is the death of a child. When sickness attacks our body, the fear that grips us is usually a fear of death. This was the result of sin that entered mankind at the Fall in the Garden of Eden (Genesis 2:17). When Adam sinned, his sinless and undefiled body became corrupted and defiled with sin. Sin began to destroy man from the inside out. First it was a spiritual death. Adam lost connection with Almighty God. (We will discuss later how the power of the cross gained our victory over this separation.)

Man did not only experience a spiritual death; slowly but surely Adam's body began to decay. Adam, once vibrant and healthy, began to feel aches and pains within his body. Sickness and disease would set in. His once youthful physique grew tired as the years passed on. Eventually both Adam and Eve would die. But they would both feel the sting of death much sooner in life.

I am not sure what it must have been like for Eve the day she realized the true extent of what death truly meant. The first human being actually to die was her beloved son Abel. As previously stated, a mother's worst fear is the fear of losing a child. Today we all understand that death is a part of life. We have all experienced, in one way or another, the pangs of death. But for the first family, Adam and Eve, they had never experienced death. There simply was no precedent for this. At this point the true fear of death entered into the heart of man. This day would be the day they experienced the sting of death for the first time, and let me tell you, it must have been an overwhelming grief.

Here, at Abel's funeral, the devil chained us with the fear of death. As sin spread like a virus, corruption took control of the mind of man, more violence ensued and with it more death. I suppose as Eve nurtured a sick grandchild, she could still feel the sting of the death of her son Abel. No doubt she trembled with fear that this child could die as well.

Anyone who has experienced the death of someone very close will understand the pain associated with death much more than others. When I was young, we lived not far from a large cemetery. It had many large monuments and manicured roads, situated in a well-to-do part of a Chicago suburb. We would climb the large statues and ride our bicycles through the freshly cut grass. I do remember feeling a small bit of reverence for the deceased but not enough to keep me from playing on the large headstones. I remember reading the names on the tombstones, but it was simply out of curiosity, like reading information about men and women who once lived out of a history book at school. But all that has changed.

When I was in my early twenties, my wife and I were just getting started in life as a family. Our first son, Dustin, was eighteen months old when she gave birth to twin boys, Payton and Clinton. On the days leading up to the birth of the twins, we were excited about the future of our family. But something had gone terribly wrong. During the pregnancy, unknown to anyone, the babies suffered from twin-to-twin transfusion syndrome, resulting in Clinton being born severely handicapped and fighting for his life. Clinton fought a long battle for eight months until he finally passed away in the night at our home.

There are really no words to describe the surreal feelings that death brings to an individual. This was, for me, an awakening of fear that had never existed. The defeat of death had inflicted its sting into my heart. Our family was almost torn apart after this tragic event. I was not a believer at the time; in fact, I was still an atheist. Therefore, I had no peace in the Christian hope of life eternal. I am thankful that God revealed Himself to me at the cross of my personal conversion and miraculously healed our wounds and restored my broken family. Details of this event are laid out in my book, *I Was an Atheist: But God.*

My trips to the graveyard feel much different now than they did when I was a child. Now, as I walk through the rows of tombstones, I remember the day I came as a mourner. I stop and read the names, but now, I ponder the question, "Who might this deceased person have been?" This was someone's son or daughter. They could have been a father or a mother. I imagine the family all gathered around this very spot on the day they laid the loved one to rest. How much grief was experienced? Some mother, brother, wife . . . would never be the same.

I wonder if they were ready to meet death's chamber, if they were ready to meet their Maker and their Judge. I am now very careful not to step on the resting place. I make certain not to move or touch anything in fear of disturbing this sacred place. When you experience the defeat of death's blow in your life, you are never the same. Death leaves a mark upon your heart that nothing can take away.

To the nonbeliever, death leaves many unanswered questions. There at death's chamber the atheist feels the most frustration about his beliefs or, should I say, lack of faith. The day I laid my son to rest, I was more fearful than I had ever been. Terrified would be a better word to describe those feelings. I remember being at the viewing. My wife and I had some time alone with our son in the viewing room. We talked about how much he had blessed our lives. We commented on his beautiful hair and his wonderful smile.

After a long while, my wife suggested that it was time to leave. As we turned to walk out of the room, I was gripped with fear. It is a feeling that I cannot put into words. For the first couple of months of Clinton's life, my wife was still recovering from surgery and taking care of Payton. So I stayed at Texas Children's Hospital with Clinton. I was by his side night and day. I would read to him and hold his hand. I was there with him as they poked him with everything you can think of. I was doing my very best to be a good dad for him. I told him over and over again that I would not leave him and that I would do everything within my power to keep him safe. But here, at the viewing room, I was about to leave him alone. I couldn't move.

The fear that I was leaving Clinton in the chilly hands of death was more than I could bear. My heart was crushed as I imagined the empty, cold, lifeless darkness where Clinton would spend the rest of his day. I literally fell to the ground as my legs would not allow me to walk out on him. I was in anguish of weeping and wailing. I said to my wife, "I cannot leave him alone," over and over. I could not bear it. I had promised him I would never leave him alone, and now, I was leaving him at death's pit.

My wife encouraged me to gain some composure. I can remember her lifting my arms to get me to stand. I would stand and take another two or three steps and then fall to the ground again. I imagined that after we departed they would come to close the lid on his coffin forever. Clinton would forever be locked in darkness. I am not sure how my wife got me to leave the room, but we finally walked out.

My torment did not end there. For many days and weeks after the funeral, I was haunted with nightmares and visions. I would see my son's face, in a decaying condition, coming from the darkness to get me. I was consumed with guilt that I had left my baby to the grave. I could not go outside at night alone for the fear of seeing this vision again. I remember one night I was dropping the tailgate of my pickup and I saw him coming at me from the darkness of the bed.

At this moment I realized I needed to seek professional help. For the believing Christian, the feelings that I described may seem incomprehensible. But for someone who has no hope in God and no hope in eternity, these feelings are quite "normal." At least that's what the psychiatrist told me:

"What you are experiencing is normal." We need to realize that before Calvary, we were all living without hope. Until the cross, this was the "normal" sting of death.

I can tell you from personal experience that the fear of death is horrifying, and it is truly crippling. But thanks be unto God that He did not leave us in darkness but gave us hope in eternal life.

> *O death, where is thy sting? O grave, where is thy victory? . . . But thanks be to God, which giveth us the victory [over sin and death] through our Lord Jesus Christ* (I Corinthians 15:55, 57).

Not only did Jesus defeat the devil at the cross, but He also defeated death. The fear of death is what the devil used as chains to cripple us. He used the fear of death as a leverage to enslave us.

> *That through death he might destroy him that had the power of death, that is, the devil; and deliver them who through **fear of death** were all their lifetime **subject to bondage*** (Hebrews 2:14b-15, emphases mine).

I Go to Prepare a Place

> *Simon Peter said unto him, Lord, whither goest thou? Jesus answered him, Whither I go, thou canst not follow me now; but thou shalt follow me afterwards* (John 13:36).

John 13-17 is said to be the upper-room discourse of Jesus Christ. They are the last words to His disciples before

Calvary. Here Jesus informed them that He was about to leave them. Peter asked if he could go with Jesus, but Jesus replied: "Where I am about to go, you cannot follow Me now."

Peter did not yet understand these words, but Jesus was on a journey to meet with death and to "go" to death's chamber. Jesus continued in this same vein of conversation into chapter 14:

> *Let not your heart be troubled: ye believe in God, believe also in me. In my Father's house are many mansions: if it were not so, I would have told you. I go to prepare a place for you. And if I go and prepare a place for you, I will come again, and receive you unto myself; that where I am, there ye may be also. And whither I go ye know, and the way ye know* (John 14:1-4).

Jesus was telling them that dwelling places were reserved for them in heaven (the Father's house). But work needed to be done at the cross in order to prepare a way for them to reach their heavenly home. "I go to prepare a place" was not referring to Jesus' need to finish some construction project in heaven. The "mansions" or, better translated, dwelling places, were already finished. Verse 2, "In my Father's house ***are*** many mansions." Jesus spoke in the present tense, indicating the dwelling places were in existence.

If Jesus had spoken these words at Bethany, after the Resurrection, we might think that He needed to go to heaven and make our dwelling places ready. But we know, at the time of this dialogue, He was going instead to meet death. If Jesus did not go to the cross, there would be no way possible for us to make it to heaven.

Hengstenberg notes this:

In what way did our Lord provide a place for His people? He tells us Himself, in John 16:10. By His departure to the Father He obtained that righteousness which is the essential condition of entrance into the Father's house. By the propitiatory virtue of His sacrifice of His life for the sheep, John 10:11, the partition between heaven and earth was done away. Eternal life was won, when Christ, the antitype of the brazen serpent in the wilderness, took sin upon Himself, and expiated it as a substitute, John 3:15. But with the atoning sufferings there was connected, in order to the preparation of heavenly places, the resurrection and ascension of the Redeemer. He must first enter as our *gr* - pro/dromo, our Forerunner, into eternal glory, Heb 6:20. The Head must be in heaven before the members can enter there. To be in heaven is to be with Christ. We can conceive of the glory of believers only as the participation in His glory, as their assumption into glorious fellowship with Him.

Our entrance into the glory of heaven being thus made so entirely dependent upon Christ, His atoning sacrifice and entrance into glory, it follows, that in the times before the Christian economy this entrance was not fully opened, and that the pious of the Old Testament were only in a state of preparation. Christ first perfectly abolished death, and brought life and immortality to light, 2 Tim 1:10. The paradise in which, according to Luke 23:43, the penitent thief was to be with

Christ, was opened first by Him.[3]

What Jesus was telling the disciples was this: "I promise you, there are dwelling places for you in heaven. But right now, you cannot get there because death will hold you forever. I have to go to the grave so I can get the keys to death's door and pave a way for you to come out the other side. If I go to the grave, do not worry, because death cannot hold Me. The grave cannot keep Me, and I will assuredly come back for you. And after I have victory over death, you will then be able to join me in My Father's house. Furthermore, after I go away I will not leave you alone, but I will send My Spirit to be with you. . . . But none of this can happen unless I go to prepare access for you to pass through death."

The Trojan Horse

The Trojan horse is a story from the Trojan War. After a ten-year siege, the Greeks constructed a huge wooden horse. Inside this hollow cocoon, they placed a squad of mighty warriors. The Greeks then pretended to leave the battle and sail away. Curiosity got the best of the Trojans. At nightfall, the Trojans pulled the horse into their city as a victory trophy. That night the Greeks hidden inside slipped out and opened the gates from the inside. The Greeks entered and destroyed the Troy, ending the war. "None of the rulers of this age knew the wisdom, for if they had known it, they would not have crucified the Lord of glory" (I Corinthians 2:8, HCSB).

Just like in the Trojan siege, the devil played perfectly into the hands of a cunning God. The devil plotted the death

---

[3] *Commentary on the Gospel of John*, E. W. Hengstenberg. Biblesoft Formatted Electronic Database. Copyright © 2015 by Biblesoft, Inc. All rights reserved.

of the prophets and ensured the death of Jesus (John 8:39-44). The devil did not realize that the man Christ Jesus had escaped the corrupted bloodline of Adam and Eve (Matthew 11:27). The world did not know Jesus, only those knew to whom Jesus revealed Himself. The devil thought that if he just got Jesus into death's chamber, he would silence Him forever. This proved to be a fatal mistake for that old fox.

Jesus was a sinless man, and thus death could not hold him. "Whom God raised up, having loosed the pains of death, because it was not possible that He should be held by it" (Acts 2:24, NKJV). The virgin birth assured that Jesus would be born without the corrupted blood of Adam. Adam was the only other man who was created with a pure and sinless bloodline. Jesus is referred to as the last Adam in I Corinthians 15:45. "And so it is written, The first man Adam was made a living soul; the last Adam was made a quickening spirit." Adam was from the ground and to the ground he returned, but Jesus was not from the earth but rather from heaven (I Corinthians 15:47). The great contrast between the first Adam and the last Adam is found in Romans 5.

> *For if by the one man's trespass the many died, how much more have the grace of God and the gift overflowed to the many by the grace of the one man, Jesus Christ. And the gift is not like the one man's sin, because from one sin came the judgment, resulting in condemnation, but from many trespasses came the gift, resulting in justification. Since by the one man's trespass, death reigned through that one man, how much more will those who receive the overflow of grace and the gift of righteousness reign in life through the one man, Jesus Christ* (Romans 5:15b-17, HCSB).

Jesus was fully God and fully man, yet no sin was found in him (I Peter 2:22; Hebrews 4:15). Therefore, death could not hold him. "For the wages of sin is death" (Romans 6:23). Wages are the pay earned by a soldier for war, his stipend. So because we are sinners and we all sin, the payment due to us is death. Death is our reward for our actions and sinful state. Jesus had no sin in him from Adam's corrupted bloodline, nor did Jesus ever commit any acts of sin. Therefore, the wages of death could not be given to him. Death had no place in him.

Jesus was not only a sinless man who could not be held by death, but He had authority over death.

> *The centurion answered and said, "Lord, I am not worthy that You should come under my roof. But only speak a word, and my servant will be healed. For I also am a man under authority, having soldiers under me. And I say to this one, 'Go,' and he goes; and to another, 'Come,' and he comes; and to my servant, 'Do this,' and he does it"* (Matthew 8:8-9, NKJV).

The centurion had a great revelation that was unsurpassed in all of Israel about the authority of Jesus over sickness. Jesus, the Creator of heaven and earth, exercised authority over disease, nature, demons, sickness, defilement, sin, man, and even death. His ability to forgive sins was based on His ability to heal disease.

When they asked Jesus to heal the lame man in Mark 2:5, "He said unto the sick of the palsy, Son, thy sins be forgiven thee." When they questioned His authority to forgive sins, Jesus declared to them that the power He used to heal was the same power He used to take authority over sin (Mark 2:8-10). Jesus also uses this same authority over death.

In John 2:19 Jesus revealed His ultimate authority over man's greatest fear, death. He told the religious leaders that when they killed his body, He would exercise His authority over death and raise Himself from the grave. Jesus continued throughout His earthly ministry to prove this point.

Faced with the death of her brother, Martha did not understand when Jesus told her that Lazarus would live again (John 11:24). Martha, although she had faith in His ability to heal, did not have faith in Him to take authority over death (John 11:21). Death is the ultimate payment of sin. It is the irreversible outcome of sin's toll on humanity. Martha had witnessed Jesus heal the sick, but death? This was simply too big for Jesus.

> *Jesus said unto her, I am the resurrection, and the life: he that believeth in me, though he were dead, yet shall he live* (John 11:25).

Jesus just revealed His hand about His authority over death. His explanation here tells us that Jesus has not only authority over sin, sickness, and disease . . . but total authority over death. And everyone who puts his faith in Jesus will also have authority over death.

Because Jesus has authority over death, He can go to death's vaults and open the doors for all those who are bound. As He called for Lazarus to "come forth," death could not hold Lazarus any longer. Death's power was subject to Christ's authority over it. Death had no choice but to unlock the chains that held Lazarus in darkness.

This message goes much deeper than Lazarus. This message is for you and me as well.

> *Thy dead men shall live, together with my dead body shall they arise. Awake and sing, ye*

> *that dwell in dust: for thy dew is as the dew of herbs, and the earth shall cast out the dead. Come, my people, enter thou into thy chambers, and shut thy doors about thee: hide thyself as it were for a little moment, until the indignation be overpast. For, behold, the LORD cometh out of his place to punish the inhabitants of the earth for their iniquity: the earth also shall disclose her blood, and shall no more cover her slain* (Isaiah 26:19-21).

Death Is Destroyed

When Jesus was crucified and died, His Spirit entered death's chamber. There Jesus exercised total authority over death and unlocked the doors from the inside.

> *For he must reign until he has put all his enemies under his feet.* ***The last enemy to be destroyed is death****. "For he has put everything under his feet"* (I Corinthians 15:25-27a, NIV, emphasis mine).

Praise be unto God for disarming the fear of death for all those who believe! Jesus, because He was fully man, was the only man who could ever have gone into death and opened the doors for us all. He was our righteous forerunner. And everyone who follows Jesus through death's chamber will have authority over it.

> *This hope we have as an anchor of the soul, both sure and steadfast, and which enters the Presence behind the veil, where the forerunner has entered for us, even Jesus, having*

become High Priest forever according to the order of Melchizedek (Hebrews 6:19-20, NKJV).

Who has saved us and called us with a holy calling, not according to our works, but according to His own purpose and grace which was given to us in Christ Jesus before time began, but has now been revealed by the appearing of our Savior Jesus Christ, who has abolished death and brought life and immortality to light through the gospel (II Timothy 1:9b-11, NKJV).

Matthew Henry noted about II Timothy 1:10:

By the gospel of Christ death is abolished: He has abolished death, not only weakened it, but taken it out of the way, has broken the power of death over us; by taking away sin he has abolished death (for the sting of death is sin, 1 Cor 15:56), in altering the property of it, and breaking the power of it. Death now of an enemy has become a friend; it is the gate by which we pass out of a troublesome, vexatious, sinful world, into a world of perfect peace and purity; and the power thereof is broken, for death does not triumph over those who believe the gospel, but they triumph over it. O death! where is thy sting? O grave! where is thy victory? 1 Cor 15:55.[4]

---

[4]Henry, *Commentary on the Whole Bible.*

Jesus came to fulfill the curse upon the serpent in Genesis 3:15. This was the final blow to the headship of Satan. Jesus walked into the capital of the enemies' camp, with all of the fierceness and wrath of Almighty God. I can only imagine how the Trojan horse deal actually went down. I wish I could have been there when Jesus went into the grave like a lamb but arose from the pit like a lion.

I imagine Jesus looked at death in the eyes (supposing it has eyes, of course), pulled out His sword, and declared, "You have beat up My children, you have ravaged and tormented them, you have lied to them. You have turned them away from Me and caused them to curse Me and follow after other gods. You have turned My virgins into harlots, and My sons have sold their souls for power and filthy lucre. And now, for every mother who has held her dead child in her arms, for every father who was crippled under the fear of death's sting, for every man who has lost his wife . . . the pangs of death have tortured humanity for centuries . . . now I want the keys to every door, every lock on every chain. I command you, death, to fall to your knees and be rendered powerless under My command!"

I don't know, do you think my imagination a bit too dramatic? I think not:

> *And when I saw him, I fell at his feet as dead. And he laid his right hand upon me, saying unto me, Fear not; I am the first and the last: I am he that liveth, and was dead; and, behold, I am alive for evermore, Amen; and have the keys of hell and of death* (Revelation 1:17-18).

He does not hold literal keys but death's authority. The head of Satan has been crushed. Jesus took away the devil's ugly stick, used it for a cross, and then turned right around and beat death, hell, and the grave with it until they were rendered wholly ineffective.

There was so much victory over death when Jesus died that the grave began to release those who were trapped in its vaults.

> *And the graves were opened; and many bodies of the saints which slept arose, and came out of the graves after his resurrection, and went into the holy city, and appeared unto many* (Matthew 27:52-53).

By the power of God, Jesus raised himself from the dead and became our access out of the grave (I Corinthians 15:20-28). "For the Lord himself will come down from heaven, with a loud command, with the voice of the archangel and with the trumpet call of God, and the dead in Christ will rise first" (I Thessalonians 4:16, NIV).

When we follow Jesus' steps into the grave, we will have access to escape it. Death cannot hold us down. No devil on earth can condemn us to an eternal grave.

We need to follow Jesus through the grave now so that when we die we can follow Him to heaven in the rapture of the church. This is how you partake of the death, burial, and resurrection of Christ now: Repent of your sins (death to self), get buried with Christ in the watery grave of baptism in Jesus' name, and then be resurrected from the dead by that quickening Spirit of the Holy Ghost (Romans 6:1-10; Acts 2:38). Because Jesus took authority over death, He gives us the keys when we are born again of the water and Spirit (John 3:5). Being born again releases us from that old corrupted nature from Adam (Colossians 2:8-15). We are no longer children of wrath but we become the sons of God (Ephesians 2:1-5).

When a loved one passes away, we certainly still feel the pain of our loss. We may even have apprehension about the possibility of losing someone whom we love deeply. Even though Jesus has made the eternal sting of death of no effect, we still feel that sharp pain of loneliness when someone we love passes on. But I do know this: No father who puts his faith in Jesus will ever feel the horror I felt the day I thought my baby was going into death alone, to be buried for an eternity in some dark abyss. For we know that to be absent from the body is to be in the presence of our Lord (II Corinthians 5:8). One day we will put off this temporary bag of flesh and exchange it for a glorified body.

Now that I have been born again and I put my faith in Jesus Christ, I can declare to my old tormentor and enemy: "O death, where is your victory? O death, where is your sting? For you have been swallowed up in victory."

Chapter Four

Victory over Sin

> *Then the LORD said to Moses, "Make a fiery serpent, and set it on a pole; and it shall be that everyone who is bitten, when he looks at it, shall live"* (Numbers 21:8, NKJV).

Snakes are by far the most feared creatures in all of the world. Spiders, scorpions, and other creepy crawlers all have their places, but above all, the snake is the worst. Just consider the way they move, how they look, and how they eat or how they feel to the touch, so cold. I once saw a snake climbing straight up a brick wall in the corner of a house. It was a terrifying sight for me especially because I cannot stand snakes. Everything about a snake gives me the creeps. And besides that, they bite!

Snakes are not only creepy to look at, but they can be very deadly. Snake venom is an incredible substance.

There are three basic types of snake venom:

1. Hemotoxic – This affects the cardio system. First it slows the victim's heart rate and then eventually turns the blood into a gelatin-type consistency. Nice!
2 Cytotoxic – Affects the muscle groups. The victim will begin to have spasms followed by crippling

cramps, at which time the snake will eat its prey alive. In larger victims, like humans, this venom will cause severe damage to the tissue, almost like gangrene. Very nice!

3. Neurotoxic – This affects the brain. The victim will experience extreme neurological dysfunctions such as dizziness, vomiting, coma, and eventually death. Yes, aren't snakes wonderful?

As if all of this isn't bad enough, some snakes have a complicated venom that contains a mixture of two venoms in one. In addition, some snake venoms contain enzymes that react differently to different types of blood. When these enzymes come in contact with human blood, they cause a domino chemical reaction, which is sometimes so complicated that doctors do not know how to treat it.

My study on the deadliest snakes in the world has given me more information than is probably healthy for my mental state, given the fact that I cannot stand snakes. But let's go through the short list of some of these horrible vipers. These snakes are listed in order of their ranking. Ranking includes average size, venom yield and toxicity, disposition, and number of bites per year. From the web site www.reptilegardens.com, we learn of:

1. **Russell's Viper** – *Asia* – This snake is the leading cause of death in the country of Sri Lanka and on par with the common cobra for deaths in the rest of its range.

2. **The King Cobra** – *Asia* – These are the largest of all venomous snakes and are highly intelligent. It is said they can produce enough venom in one bite to kill an elephant.

3. **Coastal Taipan** – *Australia* – The venom delivered in a single Taipan bite is enough to kill up to twelve thousand guinea pigs. This is the largest venomous snake in Australia. Before antivenom was available, 100 percent of bites were fatal.

4. **Puff Adder** – *Africa* – Many legs and arms need to be amputated due to this snake's venom!

5. **Barba Amarilla** – *Central South America* – These large, aggressive snakes have long fangs and lots of very toxic venom. Members of this genus are some of the only snakes that can, and regularly do, strike more than half their body length.

The Great Dragon

Of all the deadly snakes in the world, none of these can even come close to the most deadly, wicked of all. This serpent has the worst disposition, the longest fangs, the most toxic venom, and more bites that all the other snakes. More deadly than the cobra, faster than the black mamba, and more vicious than the cottonmouth, it has claimed the lives of more than all other snakes combined. This snake is found on every continent in the world and is none other than the great dragon himself, Satan our adversary (a.k.a. the devil, the tempter, liar, and father of all lies). His venom is called sin and is injected into the bloodstream through his fangs called lies.

This serpent is sly, cunning, and smarter than any other beast in all the world. Some snakes are so cunning that they can move under a laying chicken and eat all of her eggs before she ever realizes that she is sitting on a snake. But Satan's moves are even more subtle. He can move so gently and methodically that you can literally live a lifetime and never be aware of his presence in your life. All the while he is destroying everything and everyone you love.

It is a truth that snake venom can be very toxic. But if you look closely, you will discover that it actually contains large amounts of protein that are good for the body. The devil's venom is no different. The venom of Satan is mixed with mostly truth. He speaks truth in lies. He told Eve in the Garden of Eden: "Yea, hath God said, Ye shall not eat of every tree of the garden?" (Genesis 3:1). He begins with truth and then slips in the lie. "And the serpent said unto the woman, Ye shall not surely die: for God doth know that in the day ye eat thereof, then your eyes shall be opened, and ye shall be as gods, knowing good and evil" (Genesis 3:4-5). At first glance this deadly venom appears to be good to ingest. Eve, unfortunately, believed the lie and was the first victim of this deadly viper.

This snakebite would prove to be fatal for Eve, for God said if you ever take the venom of sin, you will surely die. Eve died, and then Adam was injected with the same venom. The venom of this snakebite kills the spiritual man inside you instantly and then slowly begins to deteriorate your physical body. The venom of sin did not stop with Adam and Eve. When the woman conceives a child, the blood of that child comes from the father; therefore, every child that was born from Adam and Eve was infected as well. The children are born spiritually dead all the while the venom is killing their physical bodies slowly and methodically.

The Venom

The first sign of the venom taking its toll on the human body was the introduction of fear in the hearts of Adam and Eve (Genesis 3:10). But when Satan's venom mixed with the blood of Cain, it compounded and had a more severe effect on him. Fear turned into jealousy then moved to hatred and ultimately murder. Cain was then cast out and experienced guilt, shame, and loneliness. The snakebite had begun to take its toll on this first family in a big way. The bliss once experienced in the Garden of Eden had turned into a nightmare of pain, suffering, and death.

Satan's venom is complex in that it holds all three types of venom.

1. Hemotoxic – Cardio system. It goes straight to the heart of the victim. "The heart is deceitful above all things and beyond cure" (Jeremiah 17:9, NIV). The venom brings evil and corruption to the soul of man. Since every human action is derived from the heart, this poison brings death and destruction. Isaiah described a person who is infected with sin.

They hatch the eggs of vipers and spin a spider's web. Whoever eats their eggs will die, and when one is broken, an adder is hatched (Isaiah 59:5, NIV).

The heart produces the product of its infection. . . . Snakes breed more snakes.

2. Cytotoxic – The muscle groups (physical body). The venom first attacks the heart of man (the soul), and because the heart is corrupted, the body follows. When the heart conceives wickedness, the body reacts in anger, murder, lasciviousness, and all acts of sexual perversion. All these actions will eventually kill the man physically. All the while the active ingredient of sin is death, and the victim will die eventually from sickness, disease, or simply deterioration of the flesh (old age).

3. Neurotoxic – The brain. The victim will experience extreme neurological dysfunctions such as depression and confusion. Many victims will end up in a mental hospital where there is no cure for the effect on the brain. These hospitals can only treat the symptoms of the sin. They can never provide a cure.

Because of the mix of this deadly venom and its adverse effect on human blood, it is the sole cause of cancer, AIDS, heart disease, diabetes, black plague, Parkinson's disease, Alzheimer's, arthritis, liver disease, and every other sickness one can list. In fact, every illness that has come to mankind was caused by the venom of sin. Many people have tried to minimize the agony of the effects of this snakebite by dulling the pain with drugs and alcohol. However, this only adds to the misery of the victim's death sentence, and the human body's decision to self-destruct is a natural reaction of the venom's effect on the brain.

The venom called sin makes a person think that self-destruction can bring life. It leaves a person empty inside. An inner fear rages that cannot be calmed by any medication. This emptiness and fear drive people to divorce, adultery, and fornication of every sort. They seek any type of pleasure to ease the effects of the torturous venom running uninhibited through the bloodstream.

The venom is so great and so deadly that no one can ever escape its wrath. The victims of sin do not suffer one death but three consecutive deaths. First is the spiritual death that we are all born with. Next is the physical death that is normally the result of a slow and agonizing life full of strife, anxiety, and pain. The third and final death is where this snakebite leaves all other snakebites behind. It is the death in eternity. Anyone who dies with this venom in his veins will die for eternity.

Snakebit in the Wilderness

To illustrate the horrible effect of this snakebitten situation, the Lord sent serpents into the wilderness to bite the people of Israel. The people of Israel had been released from the clutches of Egypt's bondage. God miraculously delivered them into the wilderness, where they received lifesaving supplements every day.

The people, however, began to murmur and complain about God's provisions. They were naturally reacting to the venom that was running through their bodies. Sin will cause you to become unholy and unthankful and to curse God. So in order to show us an example of sin's effect on our lives, God sent actual snakes to bite the people.

One by one, the snakes began killing the people. It had gotten so bad that they came to Moses and asked him to pray that God would save them from these deadly snakes. The Lord responded to Moses' intercession in Numbers 21:8-9. He instructed Moses to make a brass serpent, place it on a long pole, and lift it before all the people. And whenever anyone was bitten by one of the deadly snakes, they were to look upon that brazen serpent. They would not then be affected in any way by the venom.

We Are All Born Snakebitten!

All the things that happened in the wilderness to the children of God are there for our example. "For everything that was written in the past was written to teach us, so that through the endurance taught in the Scriptures and the encouragement they provide we might have hope" (Romans 15:4, NIV).

So how do we find hope in this example? Jesus exposed this hope in John 3.

There was a man of the Pharisees named Nicodemus, a ruler of the Jews. This man came to Jesus by night and said to Him, "Rabbi, we know that You are a teacher come from God; for no one can do these signs that You do unless God is with him." Jesus answered and said to him, "Most assuredly, I say to you, unless one is born again, he cannot see the kingdom of God." Nicodemus said to Him, "How can a man be born when he is old? Can he enter a second time into his mother's womb and be born?" Jesus answered, "Most assuredly, I say to you, unless one is born of water and the Spirit, he cannot enter the kingdom of God. That which is born of the flesh is flesh, and that which is born of the Spirit is spirit. Do not marvel that I said to you, 'You must be born again.' The wind blows where it wishes, and you hear the sound of it, but cannot tell where it comes from and where it goes. So is everyone who is born of the Spirit." Nicodemus answered and said to Him, "How can these things be?" Jesus answered and said to him, "Are you the teacher of Israel, and do not know these things? Most assuredly, I say to you, We speak what We know and testify what We have seen, and you do not receive Our witness. If I have told you earthly things and you do not believe, how will you believe if I tell you heavenly things? No one has ascended to heaven but He who came down from heaven, that is, the Son of Man who is in heaven. And as Moses lifted up the serpent in the wilderness, even so must the

> *Son of Man be lifted up, that whoever believes in Him should not perish but have eternal life"* (John 3:1-15, NKJV).

When Jesus first began to talk with Nicodemus, He was not talking to him about the snakes in the wilderness. Jesus was talking to Nicodemus about the infected venom of sin that runs through the veins of every man. Jesus' explanation here tells us that we are all born snakebitten. Everything that is born from man and woman is born in sin (verse 6) and is a product of that sinful flesh. This is why Jesus tells us we must be born again (verse 3). But rather than being born again from our mothers' wombs, where we were infected in the first place, we must be born again of water and Spirit, born from a non-corrupted bloodline (I Peter 1:23). Jesus explained that everything born from man (flesh) is born snakebitten, but everything that is born from the Spirit of God is born free from the deadly venom (verse 6).

Then Jesus moved into the example from the Book of Numbers (verse 14). He reminded Nicodemus of the story in the Old Testament about the snakes killing the people in the wilderness, which Nicodemus knew very well as he was a student of Jewish law. Jesus revealed the plan that God has for everyone to become cured from this deadly snakebite from Satan. Jesus says that just like the brass serpent was lifted up in the wilderness on the pole, so shall the Son of Man be lifted up (referring to the cross). And everyone who puts his faith in Jesus will be saved from the deadly venom of that great dragon.

Oh, the Blood!

We are all born snakebitten. We are all born with deadly venom running through our veins. Nothing can be used to reverse the effects of this venom; no medicine offers a remedy. No hospital has the cure. No witch doctor can make a magic potion. No one is immune to it, but Jesus has just revealed to us that there is a cure. The "good news" or the gospel is that we do not have to die. Jesus is the only one who has the anti-venom to this horrible poison.

The making of snake anti-venom is very interesting indeed. What the doctors do is take the actual venom itself and inject it into certain types of blood. When this venom is mixed with the special blood, antibodies are formed to fight off the effects and literally kill the toxins. Many different animals are used to create anti-venom. Horses are the main donor, but lamb's blood works also. So they take the poison and inject it into the lamb's blood. After a lamb has had time to create the anti-venom, they extract the blood of the lamb, and now they have the cure.

> *For God sent Christ Jesus to take the punishment for our sins and to end all God's anger against us. He used Christ's blood and our faith as the means of saving us from his wrath* (Romans 3:25, TLB).

Jesus' blood was not affected by the Fall in the Garden. Because of the virgin birth, Jesus did not receive His blood from a fallen man. His blood came from a holy God. Mary gave birth to Jesus and He was born of flesh, yet His blood was totally pure. "But when the fulness of the time was come, God sent forth his Son, ***made of a woman***, made under the law" (Galatians 4:4, emphasis mine). Notice it said that Jesus was made of a woman, not a man and a woman.

John the Baptist introduced Jesus to a snakebitten world and said: "Behold, the Lamb of God, which taketh away the sin of the world" (John 1:29b). Nothing other than the pure blood of the Lamb can take away the sin (venom) of the world.

At the cross God injected the Lamb of God with the very venom of that great dragon. "For he hath made him to be sin for us, who knew no sin; that we might be made the righteousness of God in him" (II Corinthians 5:21). Jesus, the man who knew no sin, took into His veins the very venom of Satan. "Who his own self bare our sins in his own body on the tree, that we, being dead to sins, should live unto righteousness" (I Peter 2:24). Oh, how powerful and precious is the blood of the Lamb! When the sin of man began mixing with this precious blood of Jesus, something began to happen. His blood overcame the toxins and created the only cure for sin.

Washed in the Blood

> *For this is my blood of the new testament, which is shed for many for the remission of sins* (Matthew 26:28).

The blood of Jesus is the only thing that can reverse the effects of sin in our lives. Jesus shed His blood for our sin at the cross. So the question begs to be asked: how do we get this anti-venom applied to our lives? How can we become injected with the blood of Jesus? If we go back to the discussion that Jesus had with Nicodemus, we will see the full plan for our salvation laid out. You will remember in verses 3 and 5, Jesus said we needed to be born again, of water and of the Spirit. We also understand that we must look upon Him who has been lifted up. This would be our need to believe in Jesus Christ as the Lamb of God who can wash away our sins. Jesus went on in John 3 to tell us that we need to turn our lives to God and turn from sin (verses 16-21). This defines repentance from our sins.

Jesus says His blood is shed for the removal (remission) of sins. We are then told by Peter in Acts 2:38 that being baptized in water, calling on the name of Jesus, remits our sins. We are washed in the blood of the Lamb when we are baptized in the name of Jesus. And when we are filled with the baptism of the Holy Ghost, we are born again of the Spirit. Old things are passed away; behold, all things become new.

When you are born again, "ye are washed, but ye are sanctified, but ye are justified in the name of the Lord Jesus, and by the Spirit of our God" (I Corinthians 6:11b). That venomous snake bite from your mother's womb will have lost its eternal effect upon your life. Your mind will be conformed to the mind of Jesus. Your heart will become pure. Every sin that you have ever committed will be covered by the blood of the Lamb. "And the blood of Jesus Christ his Son cleanseth us from all sin" (I John 1:7).

The blood of Jesus literally begins to reverse every effect of the venom of sin. You will no longer need to fill your life with drugs or alcohol, for your peace will come from the Lord. People are delivered from depression and mental disease. And best of all, you will no longer face that eternal death but will receive the promise of life eternal in the very presence of your Savior.

A New Race

> *The cross is the lightning rod of grace that short-circuits God's wrath to Christ so that only the light of His love remains for believers* (A. W. Tozer in *The Old Cross and the New*).

Through the power of the cross, we are cleansed of this horrible snakebit condition. Anyone who asks if he can make it to heaven without going through the cross of Jesus

Christ is totally missing the point of what the cross has done for us. Without the shedding of blood there simply is no remission of sins (Hebrews 9:22). The cross gives us access to this new bloodline of Jesus Christ. Adam was the father of the human race, but Jesus is the Adam of a new race.

> *But Christ has indeed been raised from the dead, the firstfruits of those who have fallen asleep. For since death came through a man, the resurrection of the dead comes also through a man. For as in Adam all die, so in Christ all will be made alive. But each in his own turn: Christ, the firstfruits; then, when he comes, those who belong to him* (I Corinthians 15:20-23, NIV).

A new human race, if you will, has been established with the bloodline of Jesus. Those who are born again are born from an uncorrupted man (Jesus Christ). "Therefore, if anyone is in Christ, he is a new creation; the old has gone, the new is here!" (II Corinthians 5:17, NIV). We are new creatures, we have a new father, and our spiritual DNA has come from the Holy Spirit.

Paul explained it this way:

> *That at that time you were without Christ, being aliens from the commonwealth of Israel and strangers from the covenants of promise, having no hope and without God in the world. But now in Christ Jesus you who once were far off have been brought near* ***by the blood of Christ****. . . . Now, therefore, you are no longer strangers and foreigners, but fellow citizens with the saints and* ***members of the household***

> *of God* (Ephesians 2:12-13, 19, NKJV, emphasis mine).

Did you get that? We have been adopted into the household of God by the blood of Jesus. "Household" is from the Greek *oikeios* meaning a relative, one belonging to one's household. The antonym of *oikeios* in the Greek is also used by Paul here to describe our state before the blood of the cross: *xenos*, meaning a stranger, or one belonging to another race, an alien. I want us to fully understand the value of the blood of Jesus. It has given us a new identity, a new birth place, and a new creed. Our heritage is no longer derived from sin but of holiness. Our forefathers are not the ones listed in www.familytree.com; they are listed in Hebrews 11 and written in the oracles of faith in heaven.

When you were baptized in Jesus' name and filled with the Holy Spirit, you received a new past and a new future. "But as many as received him, to them gave he power to become the sons of God" (John 1:12). You now have privileges that are only afforded to those who are called the sons of God.

> *For ye received not the spirit of bondage again unto fear; but ye received the spirit of adoption, whereby we cry, Abba, Father. The Spirit himself beareth witness with our spirit, that we are children of God: and if children, then heirs; heirs of God, and joint-heirs with Christ; if so be that we suffer with (him), that we may be also glorified with (him)* (Romans 8:15-17, ASV).

I will not go through the list of our inheritance, for that would consume another book entirely. But we do need to become aware that when we are born again we are not simply born into a church family. There is a supernatural transformation that begins to unfold within our innermost being. It begins at the very core of our existence and flows through every part of our lives. This divine thing that takes place in us is accomplished by the blood of Jesus Christ and nothing else. It is the power of the blood that transforms us, makes us, keeps us, and draws us to God.

Obligated by the Blood

I believe that if we became persuaded of these simple truths, we would live a much greater and more victorious life. When I say victorious I mean that we would struggle a lot less with temptation or the call to worldliness. The blood calls us to holiness and nothing else. First of all, we must understand that once we have been born again (Acts 2:38) we have a divine bloodline. The privileges that are awarded to us should give us great joy, but they should also carry a great responsibility. John insists that because of the blood of Jesus, we should not walk in darkness any longer (I John 1-2). If we truly understood that we have become new creatures, I believe that we would make a greater effort to walk according to the grace that has been bestowed upon us. When I say "according to," what I mean is: to live in equal, reciprocating value of the grace of God.

We are obligated by the blood. Paul stated in the Book of Romans:

> *So then, brethren, we are **under obligation**, not to the flesh, to live according to the flesh —for if you are living according to the flesh, you must die; but if by the Spirit you are putting to death the deeds of the body, you*

> *will live. For all who are being led by the Spirit of God, these are sons of God* (Romans 8:12-15, NASB, emphasis mine).

The value of the blood of Jesus is beyond measure to all who are sinners. But to those who have been covered by His blood, set free by His blood, and delivered unto a new race by His blood, . . . the value just went to a whole new level. The blood has paid our ransom to set us free. A person was once quoted: "He paid a debt that He did not owe because we owed a debt that we could not pay." Oh, the blood! How wonderful and precious is the blood of Jesus! All the epistles are dedicated to teaching us to live according to the grace of God. Our response to Christianity should be according to or of equal value to the cross.

In the Old Testament people lived under the law of Moses. In that law were ordinances that foreshadowed the blood shed by Jesus on Calvary. These ordinances included the shedding of innocent blood of bulls, goats, and doves. These sacrifices were made because of the sins of Israel. When someone disregarded the law, in some cases, he would be stoned to death. The transgression against the innocent blood of animals was justified because of the due punishment for humans (Hebrews 10:26-28).

The writer of Hebrews stated:

> *How much worse punishment, do you think one will deserve who has trampled on the Son of God, regarded as profane the blood of the covenant by which he was sanctified, and insulted the Spirit of grace? For we know the One who has said, Vengeance belongs to Me, I will repay, and again, The Lord will judge His people. It is a terrifying thing to fall into*

> *the hands of the living God!* (Hebrews 10:29-31, HCSB).

It is not like it was under the law. We simply cannot bring the blood of Christ to the Tabernacle each time we sin. Jesus died only one time, and His blood is sufficient for our atonement. If we fail in our Christian walk—and we will fail—we have the privilege as children of this new race to be forgiven of our sins. That is the grace of God. But we are certainly obligated to grace not to sin willfully, knowing that the blood can cleanse us again (Romans 6:15; Hebrews 10:26). That would not be failing as a Christian but rather turning from Christ.

> *For it is impossible to renew to repentance those who were once enlightened, who tasted the heavenly gift, became companions with the Holy Spirit, tasted God's good word and the powers of the coming age, and who have fallen away, because, to their own harm, they are recrucifying the Son of God and holding Him up to contempt* (Hebrews 6:4-6, HCSB).

This passage of Scripture is in no way suggesting that a backslider cannot repent from sins and be renewed again. See the notes of Daniel L. Segraves on Hebrews 6:4-6.

> These verses have struck fear in the hearts of many; some have even succumbed to hopelessness after they turned from Christ back to a life of sin. But the point of verses 4-6 cannot be that it is impossible for people to be saved if they once knew Christ and then fell away from Him. Such an interpretation would fly in the face of the Atonement itself, for the blood

> of Christ was shed for the sin of the whole world. (See I John 2:2; John 1:29; Hebrews 10:12; Isaiah 53:4-12; Matthew 26:28; II Peter 3:9.) If some people—for whatever reason cannot be saved, the power of the Atonement is limited, and the blood of Jesus Christ is insufficient to atone for the sins of the whole world.
>
> Since Jesus was not only a man but also God, however, the value of His death on the cross is infinite. It is impossible for the weight of the sins of the world, no matter how despicable they are, to surpass the value of Christ's blood. The Hebrew word translated "offering" in Isaiah 53:10, in the phrase "when You make His soul an offering for sin" (NKJV), describes an offering that is more than enough to satisfy the penalty. Whatever these verses mean, then, they cannot contradict the pervasive biblical teaching concerning the efficacy of Christ's blood.[5]

We do understand, however, that once we turn away from this precious blood, there is no process, no religious ritual, there is simply no other means of finding forgiveness outside of Christ. We must, for the very blood's sake, live our lives under the shadow of the cross. That life would consist of a daily repentance and total submission to the grace of God.

Rev. Carl McLaughlin gave an illustration about a friend who was in the ministry. This man had once been

---

[5]*Hebrews: Better Things; Volume One. A Commentary on Hebrews*, Daniel L. Segraves. ©1996, Word Aflame Press, Hazelwood, MO 63042-2299; pp. 169-170.

addicted to pornography. His friend explained that he had not viewed pornography for some time yet the images of his past addiction would still come into his mind. He said that when he would close his eyes, terrible images would flash across his mind, as if he were watching it all over again. This man was eaten up with guilt and shame. Rev. McLaughlin gave his friend this advice: He told him, "The next time you see an image come into your mind, hold it there and focus on it. And when you get a really good grasp on that image—as vividly as you can—I want you to imagine the blood of Jesus as it starts from the top of the picture and runs down it until all you see is the blood." As I recall from the illustration, this ministers stopped having problems with those pornographic images. His past sin was covered by the blood of Jesus!

What keeps me on my knees in prayer? The blood.
What keeps me from committing sin? The blood.
What is calling me toward holiness? It's the blood.
What keeps my mouth from slander? The blood.
What keeps me living for God? The blood.
Why do I preach this gospel? Because of the blood!
What will get me to heaven?
Nothing but the blood of Jesus!

I Plead the Blood!

This is the reason we can never stop preaching about the blood, and we cannot ever stop singing about it. We can never stop thinking about it. The blood, like the cross, is as relevant today as it was two thousand years ago. When the devil wants to accuse you of past sins, what is your plea? You really only have two choices. First, you can plead guilty to the charges and face the consequences of your sins, which is death. Your second choice is to plead the blood. I don't know about you, but I choose to plead the blood instead of guilty. It was the cross that gave us a second choice. In fact, you can plead the blood every day.

When you begin to pray against the strongholds of the devil, the devil may ask, "How do you have authority to take dominion over me?" Your answer: "I plead the blood." Have you come to torment me before my time? Yes, I have. . . . I plead the blood.

When you pray for the sick, how do you plead? Guilty as a sinner, or do you plead the blood as a born-again child of a new "living" race, purchased by the blood of the Lamb? Yep, I plead the blood. The cross gave us access to the blood of Jesus. I am so thankful for the blood!

Here are twenty things the blood of Christ does.

1. It remits sins (Matthew 26:28).
2. It gives life to those who consume it (John 6:53).
3. It causes us to dwell in Christ and He in us (John 6:56).
4. It is the means by which Jesus purchased the church (Acts 20:28).
5. It is the means by which Jesus becomes our atonement through faith (Romans 3:25).
6. It justifies us and saves us from wrath (Romans 5:9).
7. It redeems us (Ephesians 1:7; I Peter 1:18-19; Revelation 5:9).
8. It brings those who were far away from God near to Him (Ephesians 2:13).
9. It grants us the forgiveness of sins (Colossians 1:14).
10. It brings peace and reconciliation to God (Colossians 1:20).
11. It has obtained eternal redemption for us (Hebrews 9:12).

12. It cleanses our conscience from dead works to serve the living God (Hebrews 9:14).
13. It is the means by which we enter the most holy place with boldness (Hebrews 10:19).
14. It speaks a better word than the blood of Abel (Hebrews 12:24, NIV).
15. It sanctifies us (Hebrews 13:12).
16. It makes us complete for every good work (Hebrews 13:20-21, NKJV).
17. It cleanses us from all sin (I John 1:7).
18. It bears witness in the earth along with the Spirit and the water (I John 5:8).
19. It is the means by which Jesus washes us (Revelation 1:5; 7:14).
20. It is the means by which we overcome the accuser of the brethren (Revelation 12:11).[6]

---

[6]From http://frankviola.org/2012/03/01/-thebloodofjesus/

Chapter Five

Victory over Bondage

Exodus – Part I

And as they did eat, Jesus took bread, and blessed, and brake it, and gave to them, and said, Take, eat: this is my body. And he took the cup, and when he had given thanks, he gave it to them: and they all drank of it. And he said unto them, This is my blood of the new testament, which is shed for many (Mark 14:22-24).

We need to grasp two fundamental truths in order to move into the other aspects of the study of the cross. Our full understanding depends on our comprehension of these. The first is that everything Jesus nailed to the cross was swallowed up in victory. The second is that the only way for man to become free from his sinful condition was for Jesus to assume our role as sinners and nail that life to the cross.

Everything that we were, as sinners, Jesus had to become in order to set us free from those characteristics and actions. As we move through the rest of the study of the cross, we will be driving these points home. And as you will discover, because Jesus overcame the world, so now we can overcome the world through the cross.

We Were in Bondage

> *Jesus answered them, "Most assuredly, I say to you, whoever commits sin is a slave of sin. And a slave does not abide in the house forever, but a son abides forever. Therefore if the Son makes you free, you shall be free indeed"* (John 8:34-36, NKJV).

When we are living in our sinful, unredeemed state, we are living in the bonds of sin. The Scripture likens fallen humanity to slaves living under the harsh rule of our master-dictator the devil. (See Romans 6:20-21; II Peter 2:19; Ephesians 2:1-5.) Having obtained these chains of bondage at the Fall in the Garden of Eden, we have been subject to the rigors of a slave's life ever since.

When we live in sin, we becomes slaves to it. It controls our actions. Sin dictates our attitudes, thoughts, and desires. As much as mankind may have wanted to do good, the Bible says that evil was on the mind of man continually and there was great wickedness in all the earth (Genesis 6:5). There is no escape from it.

Many men tried to live holy lives, but the chains of sin would inevitably drag them into the depths of despair. Samson, David, Solomon, and even Moses have felt the chains of sin around them.

The apostle Paul said it like this:

> *But I see another law in my members, warring against the law of my mind, and bringing me into captivity to the law of sin which is in my members. O wretched man that I am! Who will deliver me from this body of death?* (Romans 7:23-24, NKJV).

Paul said when he wanted to good, evil was present (verses 16-20). Paul insisted that he was like a slave who was sold under sin (verse 14).

God wanted desperately to save His children from the bondage of sin. Therefore, God had to become like us in order to deliver us from bondage.

> *Inasmuch then as the children have partaken of flesh and blood, He Himself likewise shared in the same, that through death He might destroy him who had the power of death, that is, the devil, and release those who through fear of death were all their lifetime subject to bondage* (Hebrews 2:14-15, NKJV).

God not only needed to become flesh but ultimately had to become like us in our sinful, fallen state. " 'He himself bore our sins' in his body on the cross, so that we might die to sins and live for righteousness; 'by his wounds you have been healed' " (I Peter 2:24, NIV).

We will continue to study the cross with this concept in mind. Each chapter will illuminate the fact that nothing happened at Calvary by accident or by chance. God designed the smallest details of Jesus' life and His death in order that we might be set free.

Egyptian Bondage!

As stated in the previous chapter, everything that is recorded in the annals of the Old Testament books is there for us to have a greater revelation of Jesus Christ. These ancient writings are, as Paul described, our schoolmaster to bring us to Christ (Galatians 3:24). The word "schoolmaster" is from the Greek word *paidagwgo*, meaning a leader, escort. Among the Greeks and Romans the name was applied to trustworthy slaves who were charged with the duty of supervising the life and morals of boys belonging to the better class.[7] So the mosaic law was not the teacher, only the guide to bring us to the teacher. The teacher is Christ.

The Old Testament is filled with types and shadows of greater things to come. God oftentimes uses the physical to illuminate the spiritual. There is no better story in all of the Old Testament that is a type of our spiritual bondage than that found in the Book of Exodus. The word "exodus" means "going out." In the situation of the Israelites, it means their "great escape." This event would prove to become the foundation, if you will, of their faith in God to deliver them from any type of hardship for years to come. God would make sure that they never forgot the day He set them free from the harsh yoke of Egyptian bondage.

To get a better understanding of how the people of God ended up in slavery, you should stop here and read the Book of Genesis 37-50. To give a brief history, I will begin with Father Abraham.

Abraham was chosen by God to be the father of a great nation (the nation of Israel). God told Abraham that He would lead him to a land of promise and that land would be an inheritance for this nation forever. (See Genesis 14-17.) Abraham's grandson would ultimately be named Israel.

This man, Israel, would be the inheritor of this land of promise and of all the other great blessings that God had promised to Abraham's lineage. Israel had twelve sons. These twelve sons would eventually make up the twelve tribes of Israel. One of these sons, the obvious favorite of his father, was named Joseph.

---

[7] *Thayer's Greek Lexicon*. PC Study Bible formatted Electronic Database. Copyright © 2006.

Joseph was hated by his brothers. In a diabolical plan to rid themselves of Joseph, they sold him as a slave into Egypt. The hand of God was upon Joseph, and through a series of miraculous events, he found favor in the eyes of the pharaoh. Joseph was promoted from slavery to Pharaoh's palace. He became second in command over all of the kingdom. During this time there was a great famine in the land. People came to Egypt from everywhere to seek refuge and the food Joseph had stored in the previous years.

Eventually even Joseph's father (Israel) and all of his brothers fled the land of promise to find food in Egypt. There the descendants of Abraham were all reunited. And in Egypt they settled and began to grow as a nation. Now, that was a brief history, to be sure!

The Book of Exodus begins with this statement:

> *Now there arose a new king over Egypt, who did not know Joseph. And he said to his people, "Look, the people of the children of Israel are more and mightier than we; come, let us deal shrewdly with them, lest they multiply, and it happen, in the event of war, that they also join our enemies and fight against us, and so go up out of the land." Therefore they set taskmasters over them to afflict them with their burdens. And they built for Pharaoh supply cities, Pithom and Raamses* (Exodus 1:8-11, NKJV).

Thus began the 430 years of hard bondage in the land of Egypt. Being enslaved by Egypt was like double jeopardy for Israel. Not only were they in slavery, but they were influenced by a worldly culture and would eventually forsake their covenant with God (Jeremiah 31:32).

The children of Israel were supposed to be separated unto God for a holy purpose and a life of worship to the one true, living God. Anyone outside this purpose was considered worldly and an enemy of God. The nations of the world practiced gross idolatry and partook in every imaginable sin. Sodom and Gomorrah were likened to the land of Egypt (Genesis 13:10). Egypt, therefore, is a type of the world or, in essence, a type of sinfulness and ungodliness. God's holy nation was now enslaved by bonds of sin, trapped within the walls of worldliness, wickedness, and idolatry.

More than ten generations of families were born in slavery in more than four hundred years in captivity. That is twice as long as America has been formed. Year after year, the people of God cried out. With every whip that snapped across their backs, a cry would go forth. For every brick lifted that crushed the back of an old woman, another wail went forth. As another son was killed and a daughter was raped by Egypt, another cry would go forth.

> *And the children of Israel sighed by reason of the bondage, and they cried, and their cry came up unto God by reason of the bondage. And God heard their groaning, and God remembered his covenant with Abraham, with Isaac, and with Jacob* (Exodus 2:23b-24).

God heard their cry and sent them a deliverer, Moses.

The Passover Lamb

> *And the goat shall bear upon him all their iniquities unto a land not inhabited: and he shall let go the goat in the wilderness* (Leviticus 16:22).

Again, for the full story refer to Exodus 1-12. God called Moses to Mount Sinai and gave him instructions to tell Pharaoh to let His people go free. Moses was then instructed to lead the nation of Israel out of Egypt and bring them back to Mount Sinai, where they would once again be restored to worship God.

Moses, obeying the command of the Lord, went to Pharaoh and demanded that he let the captives free or face the consequences of Almighty God. Pharaoh was stubborn and refused to comply. After nine disastrous plagues inflicted upon the land and the people of Egypt, Pharaoh refused to budge. This, of course, was all in the plan of God. Scripture tells us that it was God who hardened the heart of Pharaoh.

> *But the LORD said to Moses, "Pharaoh will not heed you, so that My wonders may be multiplied in the land of Egypt." So Moses and Aaron did all these wonders before Pharaoh; and* ***the LORD hardened Pharaoh's heart, and he did not let the children of Israel go out of his land*** (Exodus 11:9-10, NKJV, emphasis mine).

God was about to unfold His plan for their escape from bondage. Remember, all these events ultimately lead us to Christ.

After the ninth plague, God told Moses there would be one final plague upon the land of Egypt. This tenth plague would the most devastating of all, when God Himself would enter the city of sin and pour His unyielding wrath upon its inhabitants. The Lord said, "I will pass through Egypt and strike down every firstborn of both people and animals, and I will bring judgment on all the gods of Egypt. I am the LORD" (Exodus 12:12b, NIV). This was no "death angel" that was sent; this was God Himself.

See notes from Jamieson, Fausset, and Brown on Exodus 11:4.

> Will I go out—language used after the manner of men. But it is designed to intimate that, in the execution of this dreadful judgment which yet impended over Egypt, God would, as it were, throw aside the veil of nature, and with his unbared arm directly inflict the fatal blow. The preceding plagues had been brought on through the instrumentality of Moses and by the wave of his rod. This last plague, which was to strike a decisive blow, was not to be inflicted through human agency, or by the employment of material means, but to proceed directly from the judicial hand of God.[8]

Let's get the full picture here; God's chosen people have been beaten, bruised, and abused by the pharaoh for over four hundred years. Now was payback time. God was coming Himself to cast judgment on the sinners of Egypt, for the sake of their oppression. Sound familiar? If Egypt is a type of sin, Pharaoh is a type of Satan. God Himself is coming to crush the head of the devil and to render him totally useless. Remember, this is a shadow of better things to come.

This judgment would affect not only Egyptians but everyone who lived in Egypt, including the Israelites. So God instituted the plan for their escape through what is called the Passover. See Exodus 12 for the details of this event. God instructed Moses to have every family kill a spotless lamb. Each family would need to eat all of the meat of the lamb.

---

[8] *Jamieson, Fausset, and Brown Commentary*, Electronic Database. Copyright © 1997-2014.

Furthermore, they were instructed to take the blood of the lamb and spread it over their doorpost so that whoever walked into that household would be "covered" under the blood of the lamb. Therefore, this family would be exempt from the harsh judgment of God. The judgment would literally "Pass-over" that house, and their lives would be spared.

It certainly does not take an experienced Bible theologian to see the similarities between this Passover lamb and the real Lamb of God, Jesus Christ. And this is not by accident either; "for indeed Christ, our Passover, was sacrificed for us" (I Corinthians 5:7, NKJV).

See Matthew Henry's notes.

> The paschal lamb was typical. Christ is our Passover, (1 Cor 5:7). Christ is the Lamb of God, John 1:29; often in the Revelation he is called the Lamb. It was to be in its prime; Christ offered up himself in the midst of his days, not when a babe at Bethlehem. It was to be without blemish; the Lord Jesus was a Lamb without spot: the judge who condemned Christ declared him innocent. It was to be set apart four days before, denoting the marking out of the Lord Jesus to be a Savior, both in the purpose and in the promise. It was to be slain, and roasted with fire, denoting the painful sufferings of the Lord Jesus, even unto death, the death of the cross. The wrath of God is as fire, and Christ was made a curse for us. Not a bone of it must be broken, which was fulfilled in Christ, John 19:33, denoting the unbroken strength of the Lord Jesus.
>
> 2. The sprinkling of the blood was typical. The blood of the lamb must be

sprinkled, denoting the applying of the merits of Christ's death to our souls; we must receive the atonement, Rom 5:11. Faith is the bunch of hyssop, by which we apply the promises, and the benefits of the blood of Christ laid up in them, to ourselves. It was to be sprinkled on the door-posts, denoting the open profession we are to make of faith in Christ. It was not to be sprinkled upon the threshold; which cautions us to take heed of trampling under-foot the blood of the covenant. It is precious blood, and must be precious to us. . . . The solemn eating of the lamb was typical of our gospel duty to Christ. The paschal lamb was not to be looked upon only, but to be fed upon. So we must by faith make Christ our own; and we must receive spiritual strength and nourishment from him, as from our food, see John 6:53, 55. It was all to be eaten; those who by faith feed upon Christ, must feed upon a whole Christ; they must take Christ and his yoke, Christ and his cross, as well as Christ and his crown. It was to be eaten at once, not put by till morning. To-day Christ is offered, and is to be accepted while it is called to-day, before we sleep the sleep of death. It was to be eaten with bitter herbs, in remembrance of the bitterness of their bondage in Egypt; we must feed upon Christ with sorrow and brokenness of heart, in remembrance of sin. Christ will be sweet to us, if sin be bitter. It was to be eaten standing, with their staves in their hands, as being ready to depart. When we feed upon Christ by faith, we must forsake the rule and

> the dominion of sin; sit loose to the world, and everything in it; . . . The Jews were very strict as to the Passover, so that no leaven should be found in their houses. It must be a feast kept in charity, without the leaven of malice; and in sincerity, without the leaven of hypocrisy. It was by an ordinance forever; so long as we live we must continue feeding upon Christ, rejoicing in him always, with thankful mention of the great things he has done for us.[9]

The Great Escape

As noted in Henry's commentary above, everything that the Passover lamb did for Egypt our Passover Lamb, Jesus, does for us. The Passover lamb of Moses was killed and its body was broken so that the people of Israel could walk out of Egypt without sickness or weakness. The lamb became their sin, their weakness, their failure, their shame . . . and it died instead of them. Judgment was passed from the Israelites to the sacrificial lamb. That is what a sacrifice does, it takes the place of something or someone else. A sacrifice will become the substitute and pay the necessary penalty for the person sacrificing it.

Animal sacrifices had been in God's plan since the Fall in the garden when God covered the sins (nakedness) of Adam and Eve with skins from innocent animals (Genesis 3:21). This first sacrifice set the stage for all other sacrifices to follow. Our sins must be covered by the blood of the

---

[9] *Matthew Henry's Concise Commentary*. PC Study Bible formatted electronic database. Copyright © 2000, 2003, 2006.

innocent. Sacrifices continued as Abel, Noah, and Abraham offered sacrifices unto the Lord.

"And he shall put his hand upon the head of the burnt offering; and it shall be accepted for him to make atonement for him" (Leviticus 1:4). In the mosaic law we see what takes place in the sacrificial ritual. The sins of the man are transferred into the innocent animal. The animal assumes the guilt, therefore must pay the debt. Once the sins are transferred, by the laying on of the hands, the guilty man is freed from punishment. This, of course, was flawed in many ways. (See Hebrews 8-10.) It was, however, God's way of leading us to the cross.

Apologetics Study Bible notes on Leviticus 1:4:

> In contexts that deal with sacrifices, the laying on of hands was a symbolic act in which an animal was to stand in the offender's place as a substitute. In Num 8:10,12; 27:18,23 and Deut 34:9 it appears that the purpose of the laying on of hands was to transfer the spiritual qualities of the performer to a person or an animal. One may regard the sacrificial animal either as dying in the worshiper's place or as receiving the death penalty because of the sin transferred to it by the laying on of hands.[10]

So those who were guilty of sin in Egypt passed their judgment to the lamb, who died in their place. If they were sick or feeble, the lamb became broken instead of the people; therefore, they were healed. Any brokenness in their physical bodies was strengthened (Psalm 105:37).

---

[10] *The Apologetics Study Bible*. Copyright © 2007 by Holman Bible Publishers. All Rights Reserved.

That night in Goshen, no one slept. Screams could be heard throughout all of Egypt. As one son after another fell to his death, the whole of Egypt felt the terrible wrath of God. Pharaoh was defeated and his heart, once hardened by the hand of God, was now crushed by same hand. According to the command of God, the Israelites had prepared themselves to leave Egypt. They had their sandals on their feet, their mules packed, and as much provisions as needed to head to the mountain of Sinai. Pharaoh released the prisoners, loosed the shackles, opened the slaves' quarters, and let the people go. The 430-year battle was over in one swift move of the hand of God.

Passover Fulfilled in Christ

The Lord instructed the people of Israel to remember the Passover feast always. "And this day shall be unto you for a memorial; and ye shall keep it a feast to the LORD throughout your generations; ye shall keep it a feast by an ordinance forever" (Exodus 12:14). The yearly celebration would consist of the feast and the killing of another Passover lamb. It was also instructed that the fathers needed to explain what happened in Egypt and how the Passover lamb saved them from judgment and gave them access to freedom. They were never to forget.

For some three thousand years the Passover was celebrated. At the time of this feast we find Jesus instructing His disciples to prepare a place for the Passover.

> *When the hour had come, He sat down, and the twelve apostles with Him. Then He said to them, "With fervent desire I have desired to eat this Passover with you before I suffer; for I say to you, I will no longer eat of it until it is*

> *fulfilled in the kingdom of God"* (Luke 22:14-16, NKJV).

It was the last supper before His trial and crucifixion. Jesus was about to reveal for the first time what the shadow of the Old Testament Passover was truly about.

> *While they were eating, Jesus took bread, and when he had given thanks, he broke it and gave it to his disciples, saying, "Take and eat; this is my body." Then he took a cup, and when he had given thanks, he gave it to them, saying, "Drink from it, all of you. This is my blood of the covenant, which is poured out for many for the forgiveness of sins"* (Matthew 26:26-28, NIV).

All of the shadows of this age-old feast were coming to light in the room with Jesus at the Last Supper. The broken body would be for our healing (Isaiah 53:5). Jesus, as our sacrifice, would need to become physically wounded as a way to become like us. He would then take this broken body and nail it to His cross. "With his stripes we are healed."

The Bible tells us that the stripes (beating) that Jesus received were in such horrific proportions that "his appearance was so disfigured beyond that of any human being and his form marred beyond human likeness" (Isaiah 52:14, NIV). See also Isaiah 50:6 (NIV): "I offered my back to those who beat me, my cheeks to those who pulled out my beard; I did not hide my face from mocking and spitting." It was God's plan for the Lamb to become like us in every way. For every person who has felt the pain of wounds, Jesus took the snap of the whip. He revised the penalty for our fallen nature . . . and nailed it to the cross.

Jesus Became a Slave for Us

All that the lamb did for the Israelites, the cross does for us . . . and more. It was the final blow to the head of Satan, the final plague against him. God had come to earth Himself and became not only the Judge but also the Lamb. It was like all of humanity laid our hands upon Jesus' head, and He willingly transferred all of our fallen nature into Himself.

> *But made Himself of no reputation, **taking the form of a bondservant**, and coming in the likeness of men. And being found in appearance as a man, He humbled Himself and became obedient to the point of death, even the death of the cross* (Philippians 2:7-8, NKJV, emphasis mine).

Lost humanity is like the Israelites, trapped within Egyptian bondage. We needed freedom from chains of sin. Jesus took upon Himself our slavery and nailed it to the cross.

Slaves are the property of their masters. In most cases, slaves are bought and sold like chattel. According to Exodus 21:32 the legal value for a slave's life was thirty pieces of silver. "If the bull gores a male or female slave, the owner must pay thirty shekels of silver to the master of the slave, and the bull is to be stoned to death" (Exodus 21:32, NIV). Notice that God is the one who set the price. He was in control of this from the very beginning.

Zechariah wrote prophecies concerning the Messiah, which included the exact amount that would be used to sell Jesus to the Pharisees. "So they weighed for my price ***thirty pieces of silver***" (Zechariah 11:12, emphasis mine). Fast-forward to the day Judas stood before the chief priest and we see the prophecy fulfilled to the very penny: "And said unto them, What will ye give me, and I will deliver him unto you? And they covenanted with him ***for thirty pieces of silver***" (Matthew 26:15, emphasis mine).

God had a plan that Jesus would become a slave in Israel. Joseph, sometimes referred to as a type and shadow of Christ, was sold by his brothers into slavery. He was handed into the hands of sinners, just like Jesus.

Charles Spurgeon said about Matthew 26:3-5:

> It was one of the twelve, who went unto the chief priests, to bargain for the price of his Lord's betrayal. He did not even mention Christ's name in his infamous question, "What will ye give me, and I will deliver him unto you?" The amount agreed upon, thirty pieces of silver, was the price of a slave; and showed how little value the chief priests set upon Jesus, and also revealed the greed of Judas in selling his master for so small a sum. Yet many have sold Jesus for a less price than Judas received; a smile or a sneer has been sufficient to induce them to betray their Lord. Let us, who have been redeemed with Christ's precious blood, set high store by him, think much of him, and praise him much. As we remember, with shame and sorrow, these thirty pieces of silver, let us never undervalue him, or forget the priceless preciousness of him who was reckoned as worth no more than a slave.[11]

---

[11] *Commentary on Matthew*, Charles Spurgeon. Biblesoft Formatted Electronic Database. Copyright © 2014 by Biblesoft, Inc. All rights reserved.

Throughout the Old Testament and even into the New, the Messiah is referred to as a servant or bond-slave. Again, this was planned because God heard our cry by way of our taskmaster. He saw us in chains; He witnessed the striking of the master's whip upon our backs. In every mother who has lost her son to drug addiction, the whip snaps and the cries go forth. For every pain in sickness, a cry goes forth. When fear grips our heart, the cries go forth. God heard our cry and sent a deliverer. And He sent a lamb.

The cry of humanity brought heaven down to earth when the God of heaven came down and robed Himself in flesh. He went to the synagogue, unrolled the scrolls of Isaiah, and began to read:

> *The Spirit of the Lord GOD is upon me; because the LORD hath anointed me to preach good tidings unto the meek; he hath sent me to bind up the brokenhearted, to proclaim liberty to the captives, and the opening of the prison to them that are bound; to proclaim the acceptable year of the LORD, and the day of vengeance of our God; to comfort all that mourn; to appoint unto them that mourn in Zion, to give unto them beauty for ashes, the oil of joy for mourning, the garment of praise for the spirit of heaviness; that they might be called trees of righteousness, the planting of the LORD, that he might be glorified* (Isaiah 61:1-3).

He rolled it up, looked at every man in the building, and then stated: "Today this Scripture is fulfilled in your hearing" (Luke 4:21, NKJV). This statement was not only a promise to the slaves trapped in sin but a declaration to the devil that he was about to see the wrath of God poured out upon him for all of the wrong that he has done to God's children. The day of vengeance is the day of the cross, which was the final plague against the devil. Jesus became a slave in order to set us free from slavery, and He did it at the cross.

Chapter Six

The Lamb of God

Exodus – Part II

We discussed the power of the blood of the Lamb in a previous chapter. However, it's important to note that the blood of Jesus became for all of us what the Passover lamb was for the Israelites in Egypt. Again, Jesus took upon Himself the sins of the world and therefore became our scapegoat. He died our death, and His blood sets us free from judgment. "Since we have now been justified by his blood, how much more shall we be saved from God's wrath through him!" (Romans 5:9, NIV).

Here are just some of the similarities between the Passover lamb in Egypt and Jesus:

1. Slain on the fourteenth day.
    - The Passover lamb was slain on the eve of Passover, on the afternoon of the fourteenth of Nisan, which is the first month of the Jewish calendar (Leviticus 23:5).
    - Jesus was crucified on Passover.
2. A lamb without blemish
    - The lamb had to be without blemish (Exodus 12:5).
    - Jesus was without blemish. He was sinless (I Peter 1:18-19).

3. Taken in the prime of life
   - The lamb had to be one year old, in the prime of his life (Exodus 12:5).
   - Jesus was in the prime of His life when He was sacrificed as a young adult.
4. Personal responsibility
   - Every house and each family had to have its own lamb (Exodus 12:4).
   - Every person must be responsible to apply the blood of Jesus to his or her life.
5. Four days
   - The lamb had to be brought into the house four days before the fourteenth day of the month.
   - Four days before His death on the cross on the eve of Passover, Jesus was brought into Jerusalem on a donkey.
6. No broken bones
   - The Israelites weren't allowed to break the bones of the lamb, neither during the cooking nor even during the eating (Exodus 12:46).
   - Jesus' bones didn't get broken, not during the torture and the mockery He had to endure in the moments before His death and not during His crucifixion (John 19:36).
7. No leftovers
   - The lamb had to be consumed entirely on the eve of Passover. Nothing was to remain overnight (Exodus 12:10).
   - Jesus was taken off the cross on the same evening of His crucifixion, although this wasn't customary (John 19:31).
8. First-born
   - The lamb died in place of the first-born of the Israelites.

- The first-born is the one who receives a double portion of the family inheritance. Hence, the first-born in Egypt received the inheritance due to them from sinful man, which was death. Jesus became the first-born and took our place. Now He is the first-born from the dead (Revelation 1:5; I Corinthians 15:20) and receives the Father's good inheritance. We are now joint-heirs with Christ and are treated like the first-born son (Hebrews 12:23).

9. Blood
    - The Israelites were covered under the literal blood of the lamb.
    - We are covered by blood of Jesus.
10. Freedom given
    - The lamb opened a way to freedom from Egypt.
    - Jesus' sacrifice opens for us the way of freedom from sin.

As you can see, the list could go on and on.

If you look into the wilderness journey, almost every part of it was a figure of the coming Messiah. Everything pointed toward Calvary. In the wilderness Jesus prefigured all of the following and more:

1. The Passover Lamb.
2. The judgment of God to sinners.
3. The law given at Mount Sinai.
4. The Rock from which water flowed.
5. The well the nobles sang to.
6. The serpent on the pole.
7. The Tabernacle in the wilderness.
8. The altar of sacrifice.
9. The sacrifice itself.

10. The showbread, incense, lighted candlestick, and the laver of water.
11. The high priest and the blood sprinkled over the mercy seat.
12. The glory of God manifest.
13. The veil that separated the Holy of Holies within the Tabernacle.
14. The ark of the covenant, the mercy seat, the law of Moses, the manna from heaven, and Aaron's rod that budded.

Again, this list could go on and on. For further study on the shadows of Christ in the Old Testament refer to the books of Genesis to Malachi. "Search the scriptures; for in them ye think ye have eternal life: and they are they which testify of me" (John 5:39).

The Bruised Vine

The age-old way to get fruit trees that are not yielding fruit to do so is called cincturing. Cincturing is the process of cutting a ring of bark around the base of tree. Ancient Asia used a similar method by flagellation, that is, beating the branches and the trunk. If the tree is fully mature and has yet to yield a good crop, striking and bruising it will cause it to react to the distress, and thus the tree will bear fruit. They would also drive rusty nails into the base of the tree to cause the same effect. It is said that the fruit produced by the trees that have been flogged have a much richer and sweeter taste.

The physical creation mirrors spiritual concepts in many ways. Romans 1:20 declares that nature was God's first evangelist that testified of the glory of God. I believe God created all things to center on Him, His plan, and His children. Creation bows to His command. It is amazing how everything

God created obeys His voice without question or rebuttal, expect for mankind. Nature itself was moved when its Creator hung lifeless on the cross (Luke 23:44-45; Matthew 27:51). The sky turned dark, the rocks burst into pieces, and the ground quaked. Creation is aware of the presence of God. The Lord used many physical illustrations—from fig trees and soils to mustard seeds and weeds—to teach spiritual truths.

Jesus said:

> *I am the true vine, and My Father is the vinedresser. Every branch in Me that does not bear fruit He takes away; and every branch that bears fruit He prunes, that it may bear more fruit. You are already clean because of the word which I have spoken to you. Abide in Me, and I in you. As the branch cannot bear fruit of itself, unless it abides in the vine, neither can you, unless you abide in Me* (John 15:1-4, NKJV).

Jesus used fruit trees as a way to teach a spiritual truth. He described Himself as the vine or the root. This would also be considered the main trunk of the tree, and His church as the branches. He gives us the illustration that our Creator, the Father, is the farmer. The farmer, therefore, cares for the vineyard. He takes care to make sure His tree is producing fruit, insomuch that He will prune its branches and employ every conceivable method to make sure this vine produces its fruit. The vine is Jesus, and whoever is connected to this vine will ultimately be under the care of our great God the Father. The only branch that can bear any spiritual fruit is the branch connected to the vine in the Father's vineyard.

Just like the lamb in Egypt needed to be mature and the fruit tree should be fully mature, Jesus had approached the age of thirty years. According to Jewish custom, a man was fully mature at age thirty. This vine was healthy and fully developed. It was time for Jesus to bear His fruit. And so God began the cincturing process. Our Great Vine was tied to the whipping post, and the flagellation of the root began. It was through the beating of the vine that the great fruit of the Spirit was given through the branches of the church. As God bruised His vine and drove nails into its base, healing virtue began to flow from the root into the branches.

The prophet Isaiah gave us this popular passage about how God has lifted our sickness, carried away our sorrows, and healed us by His stripes (Isaiah 53). But let's take a look at it from the perspective of a bruised vine.

> *Who hath believed our report? and to whom is the arm of the LORD revealed? For he shall grow up before him as a tender plant, and as a root out of a dry ground: he hath no form nor comeliness; and when we shall see him, there is no beauty that we should desire him.*

Notice the chapter begins by giving the illustration that Jesus will grow up to maturity as a plant from a tender child. "Unto us a child is . . . given" (Isaiah 9:6) as a root. Even though this Messiah began as a tender plant, make no mistake that His roots are deep and connected to the power of a living God.

> *He is despised and rejected of men; a man of sorrows, and acquainted with grief: and we hid as it were our faces from him; he was despised, and we esteemed him not. Surely he hath borne our griefs, and carried our sorrows: yet we did esteem him stricken, smitten of God, and afflicted.*

Surely He hath borne (lifted off) our griefs (sickness) and carried away our sorrows (pain induced by disease). This is the power of the bruised vine. We witnessed this vine being stricken or beaten, and then Isaiah told us that it was none other than the Vine-dresser Himself striking the vine: "smitten of God, and afflicted" or humbled.

> *But he was wounded for our transgressions, he was bruised for our iniquities: the chastisement of our peace was upon him; and with his stripes we are healed.*

Through the cincturing of the vine we have healing virtue. He was bruised for our sins; by this flagellation we are healed.

> *All we like sheep have gone astray; we have turned every one to his own way; and the LORD hath laid on him the iniquity of us all. He was oppressed, and he was afflicted, yet he opened not his mouth: he is brought as a lamb to the slaughter, and as a sheep before her shearers is dumb, so he openeth not his mouth.*

Here Isaiah connected the Passover lamb and the vine. The farmer must beat the roots, tree trunk, or the branches just enough to bruise them, yet not too hard as to break them. "In one house shall it be eaten; thou shalt not carry forth ought of the flesh abroad out of the house; neither shall ye break a bone thereof" (Exodus 12:46). The Passover lamb foreshadowed the Messiah in that no bone in His body should be broken (John 19:36). God allowed the flogging of the vine just enough to accomplish the necessary bruising for fruit bearing yet not too much to destroy it.

Just like the rock that prefigured Christ, it was only supposed to be struck one time to bring forth water. Moses struck it twice. Christ was stricken once and the river opened. Now all we need to do is speak to the Rock, and the water flows (Numbers 20:11).

> *He was taken from prison and from judgment: and who shall declare his generation? for he was cut off out of the land of the living: for the transgression of my people was he stricken. And he made his grave with the wicked, and with the rich in his death; because he had done no violence, neither was any deceit in his mouth. Yet it pleased the LORD to bruise him; he hath put him to grief: when thou shalt make his soul an offering for sin, he shall see his seed, he shall prolong his days, and the pleasure of the LORD shall prosper in his hand.*

How could it please the Lord to bruise Him? The same way that the farmer can cincture a tree, knowing that it will not kill the tree but rather cause the tree to fulfill its purpose and produce fruit. Jesus continued His lesson about the vine.

> *I am the vine, you are the branches. He who abides in Me, and I in him, bears much fruit; for without Me you can do nothing. If anyone does not abide in Me, he is cast out as a branch and is withered; and they gather them and throw them into the fire, and they are burned. If you abide in Me, and My words abide in you, you will ask what you desire, and it shall be done for you. By this My Father is glorified, that you bear much fruit;*

> *so you will be My disciples* (John 15:5-8, NKJV).

If we abide in the true Vine, we will produce fruit. We are connected to the vine that has been bruised for the purpose of giving fruit to the branches. Jesus said when we are connected to this vine, we will have the power of God at our hands. When we pray for the sick, the fruit of the vine will produce healing virtue. When we pray for revival, the fruit of the vine will send the power. The Lamb of God was beaten to heal us and to set us free. By His stripes we are healed.

I also believe that everything the church has been given that is divine in its nature flows through the vine and into the branches, ultimately producing fruit. The giving of the Holy Ghost comes through the cinctured vine. The gifts of the Spirit will flow from the roots of the body to the branches, and the fruit of the Spirit will come forth.

Let's not forget that the flogging of the roots are not the only part of the tree that can be bruised to bring fruit. The branches can receive similar treatment. Make no mistake; when you are connected to the vine in your Father's vineyard, you *will* produce fruit. The Vine-dresser will not be shy to address the pruning and the cincturing needed for us as well.

> *Beloved, think it not strange concerning the fiery trial which is to try you, as though some strange thing happened unto you: but rejoice, inasmuch as ye are partakers of Christ's sufferings; that, when his glory shall be revealed, ye may be glad also with exceeding joy* (I Peter 4:12-13).

The same treatment done to Christ can be done to you. The Lord treats us like we are His sons, and the chastening and scourging that He inflicts upon us are to make us better (Hebrews 12:5-8). Being part of the Father's vineyard means being subject to all of the disciplines needed to bear fruit. The wonderful part is . . . we will bear much fruit!

In As Paupers, Out Like Kings

When the children of Israel were in bondage, they had no possessions of their own. Slaves cannot own anything, for they are owned. Everything they ever held of value was taken from them by Egypt. Not only their dignity, pride, and self-worth were stripped, but they also had no gold or silver. God not only wanted to set them free, He wanted to make sure they left Egypt decked in royal splendor. God told Moses that on the night before they left Egypt, they would take back what the devil stole from them.

> *But every woman shall borrow of her neighbour, and of her that sojourneth in her house, jewels of silver, and jewels of gold, and raiment: and ye shall put them upon your sons, and upon your daughters; and ye shall spoil the Egyptians* (Exodus 3:22).

The night they left, they took the spoils from the Egyptians. God brought them out with silver and gold, and there was none feeble among His tribes (Psalm 105:37).

The Passover turned their poverty into wealth. They were dressed like slaves, but they were leaving like kings. Let me tell you this: When God sets you free, you are free indeed. God not only made the pharaoh let them go free, but God made Pharaoh fund the trip.

In order for Jesus to change our status fully from slave to royalty, He had to take on our pauper state. In other words,

Jesus had to become poor in order to take our poverty to the cross and get victory over it.

> For you know the grace of our Lord Jesus Christ, that though he was rich, yet for your sakes ***he became poor, so that you through his poverty might become rich*** (II Corinthians 8:9, NIV, emphasis mine).

Jesus had no home where He could lay His head at night (Luke 9:58). He could have come to us as a wealthy king yet came as a servant. Jesus could have come with majesty and pomp, carried by the wings of angels, yet He came riding on the colt of a donkey. Even in His death, He could have chosen to die like a defeated king with dignity, yet He chose to hang between two thieves on a Roman cross. He had no grave to be buried in. He had only a borrowed tomb.

Jesus did all of this so that when we are set free from sin, He takes our filthy rags and clothes us with the garments of righteousness. We were once slaves, but we can become a royal priesthood (II Peter 2:9). We get to take back our dignity and self-worth. We don't walk out of prison with the clothes we walked in with. When we walk out, we are clothed with garments of praise from our Father's house. We have been given an earnest of our full inheritance (Ephesians 1:14). He found us poor slaves but makes us royal conquerors (Romans 8:37). Jesus went to the grave as a pauper, but He rose as the King of kings and the Lord of lords. When we are born again, He changes our spiritually poor status to a royal status.

I want us to understand that we are all equal at the foot of the cross. No matter who you are or how rich or poor you may be, you are equal in spiritual status when you come to Jesus. We are all poor, deep in spiritual debt; we are all owned by another master and slaves to sin.

Repentance

The Passover of Exodus opened the path for freedom to the children of Israel. It was the single event that gave them the opportunity to walk away from the sin that had them bound for so long. It manifested the grace of God for their current dilemma, and it was a shadow of Jesus' death on the cross. But the shadows of our deliverance did not end at the last plague. All this did was open the door for their escape.

When Jesus died on the cross, that was the grace of God manifest for our current dilemma, death of sin. The cross gave us an open door to walk out of sin's prison cell. Just like the children of Israel, we still have to make that choice and walk out of our Egypt. This is repentance, a turning from the sin that had us bound.

But repentance alone does not get us to full communion with God, and it certainly does not put us in the Promised Land. Nor did it do so for the children of Israel. They still had to leave Egypt and stay gone. If you read further in Scripture, the people of God continued to desire their old life in Egypt and some insisted on going back. And not only this, but the very sin that had them bound for four hundred-plus years could still kill them. Pharaoh could still come after them. . . . And, in fact, he did come after them.

God's plan for their great escape was not even close to being over. The full deliverance from the bonds of sin was just beginning. Once the children of Israel left Egypt, God led them south through the desert and into a long canyon-like gorge between two mountain ranges. Archeologists believe they can actually pinpoint the canyon where God led His people. For military purposes, this was suicide. The canyon only had one entrance. One could not climb its cliffs nor go through the other side, for there ran the deep waters of the Red Sea. Once they arrived at the Red Sea, they could not move. Fear struck their hearts as they knew that Pharaoh's army could kill them with ease. They cried out to Moses, "Were there not enough graves in Egypt that you had to bring us out here to die?"

The Bible says that God led them into a trap. They were the bait, and Pharaoh was the fox. God knew that when Pharaoh heard they had been led into this dead end, he would come after them with the intent of killing them all. And God made sure of it.

> *For Pharaoh will say of the children of Israel, "They are bewildered by the land; the wilderness has closed them in." Then I will harden Pharaoh's heart, so that he will pursue them; and I will gain honor over Pharaoh and over all his army, that the Egyptians may know that I am the LORD"* (Exodus 14:3-4, NKJV).

The sin that once had them bound could still get to them. They had repented of Egypt, but their sin was still with them, trailing them, and could still take them out. They were free but not yet fully delivered. And this was all part of God's tutor to bring us to Christ.

Born Again of Water

What the children of Israel needed was a great barrier between them and the sin that had them bound, a barrier so great that none of the sin of their past could ever haunt them. Pharaoh and the entire Egyptian army approached the Israel encampment with blood, hatred, and unbridled fury in their hearts. As they drew near, Moses calmed the people and said, "Do not be afraid. Stand still, and see the salvation of the LORD, which He will accomplish for you today. For the

Egyptians whom you see today, you shall see again no more forever" (Exodus 14:13, NKJV). Moses then stretched forth the rod, and the waters of the Red Sea parted. The children of God walked on the bottom of the Red Sea with a pillar of water on each side of them.

Pharaoh, falling right into God's trap, followed them into the Red Sea. They must have been gaining on the Israelites because God made the wheels of their chariots fall off so they would move slower. Once the children of God were clear and all of the Egyptian army was still on the floor of the Red Sea . . . God let the waters fall. "Then the waters returned and covered the chariots, the horsemen, and all the army of Pharaoh that came into the sea after them. Not so much as one of them remained" (Exodus 14:28, NKJV).

God washed all of their sins away in the watery grave of the Red Sea. God baptized them for the remission (washing away) of the sin that had them bound, leaving it in the middle of the Red Sea, never to be seen again.

> *Moreover, brethren, I do not want you to be unaware that all our fathers were under the cloud, all passed through the sea, all were baptized into Moses in the cloud and in the sea, all ate the same spiritual food, and all drank the same spiritual drink. For they drank of that spiritual Rock that followed them, and that Rock was Christ. But with most of them God was not well pleased, for their bodies were scattered in the wilderness* (I Corinthians 10:1-5, NKJV).

Jesus is our Passover lamb. His blood sets us free from sin. But we still need to repent (leave Egypt behind us) and we still need to get to the waters of baptism, where we can be cleansed from all of our sins (cross under the Red Sea). Just because Jesus died on the cross does not mean we are all automatically saved. The Passover lamb in Egypt did not automatically get them to the Promised Land. It did open the door, but the children of God still had to follow His full and complete plan of escape in order to see the reproach of their past lives in sin washed away completely. We *must* be born again of the water and of the Spirit. We cannot enter into the kingdom of God simply by believing in Jesus.

As you can see from the passage from I Corinthians listed above, the types and the shadows continue throughout the entire wilderness journey. I am not going to go through every type and shadow of the wilderness journey; that would fill yet another book. However, I do not feel I can close this chapter without reviewing one more very important event.

Born Again of Spirit

As stated above, the Passover was to be recognized every year by the Jewish people. God did not want them ever to forget the day of the slain lamb, for one day God would bring this special day into light through the cross of Jesus. But there was another day near and dear to the Lord's heart, and that was the day He gave Moses the law. You will remember from earlier in this book or from your personal Bible study that God had commanded Moses to bring His people from bondage and to bring them to the same mountain so they could worship Him. That is exactly what Moses did.

The Jewish people still celebrate the giving of the law, which is called the Shavu'ot or Festival of Weeks (Leviticus 23:15-16, 21). The time between the Jewish Passover and the Shavu'ot is a time of great anticipation. For the Jews, the Passover freed them physically but the Shavu'ot freed them spiritually from idolatry and immorality. Shavu'ot falls on the fiftieth day after Passover, so it is duly called Pentecost (as Pentecost means fiftieth). So every year the Jewish people would celebrate Passover, and fifty days later they would celebrate Pentecost (Shavo'ot). God has a plan, remember. Nothing is done by accident nor by chance. God is a God of immense detail. Just look at the intricate detail of the robes of the Levites or the building of the furniture in the Tabernacle. Everything to the very thread is detailed for a purpose.

The purpose for Pentecost was revealed for us in Acts 2. After Jesus became the real Passover lamb in Jerusalem, He instructed His disciples to go to Jerusalem and wait for the promise of the Holy Spirit (Acts 1:1-8). These 120 believers had seen Jesus raised from the dead and believed that He was the true Messiah, yet they had not been born again of the Spirit. Most of them, if not all of them, had already been baptized by Jesus (John 3:22; 4:2). So they had believed on the Lamb of God and been to the watery grave of baptism but were not born again of the Sprit. So they went to Jerusalem and found an upper room where they waited ten days.

> *And when the* ***day of Pentecost was fully*** *come, they were all with one accord in one place. And suddenly there came a sound from heaven as of a rushing mighty wind, and it filled all the house where they were sitting. And there appeared unto them cloven tongues like as of fire, and it sat upon each of them. And they were* ***all filled with the Holy Ghost****, and began to speak with other tongues, as the Spirit gave them utterance* (Acts 2:1-4, emphases mine).

God waited exactly fifty days (the same amount of days He called for in Leviticus 23:15) to send His Spirit into the New Testament church. This was the same day the Jewish nation was commemorating the giving of the mosaic law from Sinai. Coincidence? I think not. As you read through the Book of Hebrews 8-10, you will discover that the law was imperfect. Remember, Paul told Galatia that the law was simply our servant to bring us to the real teacher, Christ (Galatians 3:24). God knew that law was not perfect. It was written on tablets of stone. The law was not living inside us and therefore could not really keep us from sinning (Romans 7-8). So by the foreknowledge of God and His perfect plan for full deliverance, He gave us a promise that when the new covenant was made (that is, the New Testament) with the blood of Jesus, God would then put His Spirit in us as well.

> *Behold, the days are coming, says the LORD, when I will make a new covenant with the house of Israel and with the house of Judah—not according to the covenant that I made with their fathers in the day that I took them by the hand to lead them out of the land of Egypt, My covenant which they broke, though I was a husband to them, says the LORD. But this is the covenant that I will make with the house of Israel after those days, says the LORD: I will put My law in their minds, and write it on their hearts; and I will be their God, and they shall be My people. . . . for I will forgive their iniquity, and I will remember their sin no more.* (Jeremiah 31:31-33, 34b, NKJV).

This would be the day He would write His laws in our hearts and He would remember our sins no more. His Spirit would be within His people and through baptism their sins would be remembered no more. This was Jeremiah's description of the new covenant made by Jesus Christ. Notice also Ezekiel's description.

> *A new heart also will I give you, and a new spirit will I put within you: and I will take away the stony heart out of your flesh, and I will give you an heart of flesh. And I will put my spirit within you, and cause you to* ***walk in my statutes, and ye shall keep my judgments,*** *and do them. And ye shall dwell in the land that I gave to your fathers; and ye shall be my people, and I will be your God* (Ezekiel 36:26-28, emphasis mine).

How will we be able to keep His laws? Because of the Spirit He puts inside our hearts. These prophesies tell of the infilling of the Holy Ghost that happened on the very day the Jews were celebrating the giving of the law on tablets of stone.

And when the Jewish people asked Peter, on the Day of Pentecost, what they must do to enter the new covenant (Acts 2:37), Peter said, "Repent, and be baptized every one of you in the name of Jesus Christ for the remission of sins, and ye shall receive the gift of the Holy Ghost. For the promise is unto you, and to your children, and to all that are afar off, even as many as the Lord our God shall call" (Acts 2:38-39).

- Repentance – Turn from Egypt
- Baptism in Jesus' name – Cross the Red Sea
- The gift of the Holy Ghost – Get the law at Mount Sinai

The cross made our way of escape and this full deliverance possible. I am thankful for the cross today!

Chapter Seven

Victory over Unrighteousness

Who, being in the form of God, thought it not robbery to be equal with God: but made himself of no reputation, and took upon him the form of a servant, and was made in the likeness of men: and being found in fashion as a man, he humbled himself, and became obedient unto death, even the death of the cross (Philippians 2:6-8).

God's plan to come in the flesh could have occurred at any point in time. Knowing that He would come and be sacrificed for the sin of fallen man, He could have chosen any means of execution. He could have chosen to die by guillotine, firing squad, lethal injection, or even the electric chair. But instead, God chose to come during the first century, while Jerusalem was under Roman rule, in order to face death by crucifixion (Galatians 4:4).

If death alone was the only purpose, why didn't He die by any number of other "humane" ways? Why not keep His dignity? Why not make it quick and painless? As we will see, the details involved in the process when a person is put to death by crucifixion has many profound spiritual implications for all of us.

Stripped of His Clothing

> *Then the soldiers, when they had crucified Jesus, took His garments and made four parts, to each soldier a part, and also the tunic. Now the tunic was without seam, woven from the top in one piece* (John 19:23, NKJV).

All four of the Gospels record the fact that Jesus was hung on the cross in complete nakedness. This "tunic" refers to Jesus' undergarments that were removed just before the cross was raised. It was a common practice to strip the guilty of their clothes for crucifixion. For us to understand the spiritual purpose of this act, we must return to the original Fall in the Garden of Eden. This is when humanity entered into an unrighteous state.

If Jesus came and died on the cross the day after Adam and Eve's sin, it might be easier to connect the dots. But since there was a period of some four thousand years, it may be easy to miss the connections. What we should realize is that Jesus died on Calvary to rectify the fall of man that occurred in the Garden of Eden. When God told Eve that her child would crush the head of the serpent (Genesis 3:15), she may have thought that Cain or Abel or even Seth was the one who would bruise Satan's heal. But when the fullness of time had come, God did send forth His Son, made of a woman to take back everything the devil had stolen from us.

> *And the LORD God called unto Adam, and said unto him, Where art thou? And he said, I heard thy voice in the garden, and I was afraid,* ***because I was naked****; and I hid myself. And he said, Who told thee that thou wast naked? Hast thou eaten of the tree, whereof I*

commanded thee that thou shouldest not eat? (Genesis 3:9-11, emphasis mine).

As soon as Adam and Eve sinned, they lost their spiritual connection with God. Their prior condition of innocence gave them a righteous covering. On nine separate occasions the Bible refers to righteousness as a covering or clothing (Job 29:14; Revelation 19:8; 3:4; 7:14; Isaiah 61:10; 59:17; 11:5; Psalm 132:9; Zechariah 3:4). Without a covering, we would feel exposed, vulnerable, and naked.

Adam and Eve felt their nakedness as they lost their righteous covering and immediately tried to make some sort of clothing for themselves. "And the eyes of them both were opened, and they knew that they were naked; and they sewed fig leaves together, and made themselves aprons" (Genesis 3:7). Even though they were physically covered by these fig leaves, they still felt naked and exposed. The fear and awareness of their nakedness were rooted in the spiritual death and loss of their righteous covering.

> *But we are all like an unclean thing, and all our **righteousnesses are like filthy rags**; we all fade as a leaf, and our iniquities, like the wind, have taken us away* (Isaiah 64:6, NKJV, emphasis mine).

Isaiah spoke of our righteousness as dirty clothing. Our efforts are insufficient, just like the clothes Adam and Even sewed for themselves. Although these fig leaves may have covered them from head to toe, they still felt naked.

God, therefore, made them coats of skins and He "clothed" them (Genesis 3:21). This was the ultimate plan of God's redemption unfolding for us. God took the bloody coats of innocent sacrifices to cover the unrighteousness of

Adam and Eve temporarily. But the blood of Jesus and His sacrifice covers our unrighteousness forever, and yet another shadow of the Old Testament comes to light at Calvary.

Jesus became our mediator between a holy God and sinful man (I Timothy 2:5). Jesus took upon Himself our unrighteous (naked) state and nailed it to the cross. The stripping of the clothes at Calvary was the Lord's way of becoming like sinful man in every way. Just like Adam and Eve were naked in the garden, God became naked, exposed, and ashamed. And then He nailed that unrighteous, fallen man to the cross.

He Bore Our Nakedness

> *Jerusalem hath grievously sinned; therefore she is removed: all that honoured her despise her, because they have* ***seen her nakedness****: yea, she sigheth, and turneth backward. Her filthiness is in her skirts; she remembereth not her last end; therefore she came down wonderfully: she had no comforter. O LORD, behold my affliction: for the enemy hath magnified himself. The adversary hath spread out his hand upon all her pleasant things: for she hath seen that the heathen entered into her sanctuary, whom thou didst command that they should not enter into thy congregation* (Lamentations 1:8-10, emphasis mine).

Israel had forsaken God, and in her backslidden state, Jeremiah unfolded her demise. This chapter begins by describing Israel as a bride whose clothes have been defiled. He continued to describe Israel's sinful acts as a display of nakedness. She had exposed to the world that she was unrighteous by taking off her clothes. The details get much more explicit, but the point is that God views our sinful state as being naked. This is what happened to Adam in the garden.

The Bible has much to say about covering your physical body. God's ways are holy and righteous, and we should become desperate to live a life pleasing to Him. If you look into the holy Scripture, you will find that people who committed gross sins would strip themselves of their clothing as part of their sinful acts. Idol worship is usually played out by some sort of immodest acts, including nakedness. God certainly desires His church to be modest (I Timothy 2:9-10). There is much teaching in the Word of God about modesty in dress, and there are plenty of books you can purchase that would explain these truths in immense detail. But I will focus on just one point about modesty as it relates to the cross.

The Bible says that when they stripped Jesus of His clothing, they stared upon Him. "People stare and gloat over me. They divide my garments among them and cast lots for my clothing" (Psalm 22:17b-18, NIV). Think about this for a minute: Here we have the holy and righteous God stripped and on public display with His shame and nakedness exposed before His mother and His disciple John. The world stared at Him and gloated over Him. This was humiliation to the extreme. Jesus took our shame upon Himself to free us from our sinful state. If for no other reason than this, the church of the living God should always cover herself with modest apparel and a modest attitude. We are the body of Christ. If as the body of Christ we expose ourselves to reveal our nakedness, we bring shame and reproach to Him all over again.

We should always allow God to define for us what He considers exposing our nakedness, since we are His body. "Lift up your skirts, bare your legs, and wade through the streams. Your nakedness will be exposed and your shame uncovered" (Isaiah 47:2b-3, NIV). Running around in your birthday suit is naked; that does not need to be defined. But

God refers to "nakedness" as simply exposing your thigh. Your thigh, by the way, is that portion of leg above the knee.

Nakedness is not limited to exposing the skin. God defines nakedness in many ways, including immodest actions. So even if we cover our thighs, we could still bring shameful reproach against His body by lustful thoughts, activities, and even our attitudes. Fornication is also considered nakedness (Genesis 9:22). God uses the term "expose their nakedness" to say "expose their sexual sins" (Ezekiel 16:37). We need to understand that when we bring shame to our bodies, we are bringing the shame of the cross upon Jesus all over again. This is why Paul insisted that we abstain from sexual sins.

> *Flee fornication. Every sin that a man doeth is without the body; but he that committeth fornication sinneth against his own body. What? know ye not that your body is the temple of the Holy Ghost which is in you, which ye have of God, and ye are not your own? For ye are bought with a price: therefore glorify God in your body, and in your spirit, which are God's* (I Corinthians 6:18-20).

When we expose our nakedness in act, attitude, or dress, we sin against the body of Christ. Nakedness in all of its definitions is a sin against the body. We simply need to remember that Jesus freed us from this at Calvary, and we should never return to our nakedness in any form or fashion.

Bore Our Shame

> *Fear not; for thou shalt not be ashamed: neither be thou confounded; for thou shalt not*

> *be put to shame: for thou shalt forget the shame of thy youth, and shalt not remember the reproach of thy widowhood any more. For thy Maker is thine husband; the* LORD *of hosts is his name; and thy Redeemer the Holy One of Israel; The God of the whole earth shall he be called* (Isaiah 54:4-5).

The prophet Isaiah was illustrating the restoration of the Lord's fallen people. God took care of our shame at the cross the very same way. Verse 4 says do not fear, for you will not be ashamed. This is present tense. This includes any shame we experience in the here and the now. This promise will eliminate our fear of shamefulness. Verse 4 continues, "For thou shalt not be put to shame." This refers to any future shame that may be headed our way. The victory over sin and our new nature will eliminate our sinful actions; therefore, we will never have to be confounded or depressed because of shameful acts in our future. Verse 4 goes on to say we will forget the shame of our youth. This is past tense. Any shame that we experienced in our past will be forgotten. The blood will heal us from wounds of past sins that were done by us and done to us. Everybody who was sexually abused as a child suffers a level of shame because of these acts. I want you to know that the cross took care our shame. Again, if you do not realize the power of the cross, the devil can still throw that old shame back in your face.

We should have the heart of Paul when he said to the church at Philippi:

> *Not that I have already attained, or am already perfected; but I press on, that I may lay hold of that for which Christ Jesus has also laid hold of me. Brethren, I do not count*

> *myself to have apprehended; but one thing I do, forgetting those things which are behind and reaching forward to those things which are ahead, I press toward the goal for the prize of the upward call of God in Christ Jesus* (Philippians 3:12-14, NKJV).

The only way Paul could press forward to attain perfection was by forgetting those things which were behind. The only way Paul could press toward the mark was in letting go of his past mistakes and past shame. You will never be able to grab the prize and attain perfection if your hands are holding onto past shame. Let go, and reach forward. Release the shame from your youth and attain the prize of Christ. Paul had much to leave behind, but there was one thing he did: "forgetting those things. . . ."

Isaiah completed verse 4 by also stating that you will not remember the reproach of your widowhood any more. What is widowhood, you might ask? This is when you acted like God was dead. "For thy Maker is thine husband; the LORD of hosts is his name; and thy Redeemer the Holy One of Israel; The God of the whole earth shall he be called" (verse 5). When you acted like God, your husband, was gone, you could carry out acts of love toward another. When you lusted after other gods, you lost your righteous covering and ran around showing off your nakedness. Your very life became a reproach unto you. God said, even the shame of your widowhood you will not remember any more. This is grace at its extreme.

The story of Hosea and Gomer illustrates this point perfectly. God told the prophet Hosea to marry Gomer, knowing full well she was a prostitute. She was naked in her actions, her attitude, and her dress. Yet Hosea took her as his bride anyway. "But God demonstrates His own love toward us, in that while we were still sinners, Christ died for us" (Romans 5:8, NKJV). What an incredible God we serve! He died for us, took on our shame, and freed us of all of it: our past shame, our present shame, our future shame, and our shame against God Himself. He took it to the cross and left it there . . . forever. We are free of reproach. We are free to walk away from it. God will never bring it up again. He will never allow us to feel guilt for it. This is what Jesus did when He bore our nakedness and our shame on Calvary. Oh, what a glorious Savior we have!

Jesus Traded with Us

Clothing has been, and remains, a means of defining who we are and what roles we play. If you are accused of impersonating a police officer, what comes to mind is someone who puts on a policeman's uniform. When you see a fireman, you identify him by his clothing. Military personnel are identified by their uniform. When you dress in certain clothes, you are identified with whom it belongs to or the office which the clothing represents.

The fact that they stripped Jesus' clothes off His body was significant indeed. But what about the clothing that they took from Him? It seems that from the moment Jesus entered the time of His passion (the last twelve hours of His life), many details about His clothing surface. "And Herod with his men of war set him at nought, and mocked him, and arrayed him in a gorgeous robe, and sent him again to Pilate" (Luke 23:11). After Pilate sent Jesus to Herod, the acting king of the Jewish people, Herod robed Jesus with a gorgeous robe. No doubt since Jesus claimed to be the king of the Jews, Herod mocked Jesus by placing a king's robe on Him.

When Herod was finished, he sent Jesus back to Pilate dressed as the king of the Jews. The Romans must have followed suit with the mockery and robed Jesus with yet another set of clothing. This time it was royal purple, that which would be worn by Roman royalty.

See Adam Clarke's commentary:

> [A gorgeous robe]. It probably means a white robe, for it was the custom of the Jewish nobility to wear such. Hence, in Rev 3:4, it is said of the saints, They shall walk with me in WHITE (garments), because they are WORTHY. In such a robe, Herod, by way of mockery, caused our Lord to be clothed; but, the nobility among the Romans wearing purple for the most part, Pilate's soldiers, who were Romans, put on Jesus a purple robe, Mark 15:17; John 19:2; both of them following the custom of their own country, when, by way of mocking our Lord as a king, they clothed him in robes of state. See DR. PEARCE.[12]

> *And they clothed him with purple, and platted a crown of thorns, and put it about his head, and began to salute him, Hail, King of the Jews! And they smote him on the head with a reed, and did spit upon him, and bowing their knees worshipped him* (Mark 15:17-19).

Jesus' tunic was woven without a seam, using a single thread. Without seam (John 19:23) is defined by Strong:

---

[12] *Adam Clarke's Commentary*. Electronic Database. Copyright © 1996, 2003, 2005, 2006 by Biblesoft, Inc. All rights reserved.

> *araphos* (ar'-a-fos); This word is prefixed with the negative particle (See NT:1); According to Josephus, the high-priest's tunic was made of one piece; found only in John 19:23: seamless, without (a) seam.[13]

Jesus' own garments were those the high priest would normally wear. The tunic, next to the skin, was holy as described in the mosaic law (Exodus 39:22-23). So on the day of His crucifixion, Jesus wore the robes of the king of Israel and a Gentile king and the garments of the high priest of Israel. We should note that as Jesus wore all these clothes, the Roman soldiers bowed to Him and worshiped Him.

There was nothing done here by accident. Herod, Pilate, and the Roman soldiers acted out their desires, yet all of these details were in the plan of God. In the same way, when Pharaoh acted out his desires, he was really directed by God Himself. What Pharaoh thought was evil, God used to set His children free. What these men did to Jesus was for mockery, but God used their mockery to set His children free.

As Jesus wore the clothing of these particular offices, He assumed their identity, just as if we clothed ourselves in a police uniform. So Jesus was clothed as the king of the Jews, the king of the Gentiles, and the high priest of Israel. And he was worshiped as all three.

- "Seeing then that we have a great high priest, that is passed into the heavens, Jesus the Son of God, let us hold fast our profession" (Hebrews 4:14). **Jesus has become our high priest.**

---

[13] *New Exhaustive Strong's Numbers and Concordance with Expanded Greek-Hebrew Dictionary.* Copyright © 1994, 2003, 2006, 2010.

- "And he hath on his vesture and on his thigh a name written, KING OF KINGS, AND LORD OF LORDS" (Revelation 19:16). **Jesus is the King of every Gentile nation** over every earthly king.
- "Then Pilate asked Him, saying, 'Are you the King of the Jews?' He answered him and said, 'It is as you say' " (Luke 23:3, NKJV). **Jesus is the King of the Jews.**

Jesus took on the role of all three of the offices in the clothes he wore. But the heathen Roman guards stripped Him of all His garments. They stripped Him of His earthly king's garments and His priestly garments. They took from Him the offices that He represented and left Him naked and in shame.

> *Then the soldiers, when they had crucified Jesus, took his garments, and made four parts, to every soldier a part; and also his coat: now the coat was without seam, woven from the top throughout. They said therefore among themselves, Let us not rend it, but cast lots for it, whose it shall be: that the scripture might be fulfilled, which saith, They parted my raiment among them, and for my vesture they did cast lots. These things therefore the soldiers did* (John 19:23-24).

Here, in the acts of hateful sinners, we see the plan of redemption unfolding. These sinners did not toss these expensive clothes in the trash, but they cast lots for them. Clothing was a high commodity in these days, especially robes of royal fabric and color made with the highest quality material and labor. These sinners stripped them off Jesus and put them on themselves. They traded with Jesus their shame for His royal robes. What they did in the physical is what Jesus accomplished in the spiritual.

> *I will greatly rejoice in the LORD, my soul shall be joyful in my God; for He has clothed me with the garments of salvation, He has covered me with the robe of righteousness, as a bridegroom decks himself with ornaments, and as a bride adorns herself with her jewels* (Isaiah 61:10, NKJV).

As they wrapped His garments around themselves, they had no idea that Jesus was doing some trading with them as well.

He took their nakedness and their shame (sinful acts of mockery) and gave them garments of kings. We clothed Him in sin, and He clothed us as kings and priests.

> *And from Jesus Christ, who is the faithful witness, and the first begotten of the dead, and the prince of the kings of the earth. Unto him that loved us, and washed us from our sins in his own blood,* ***and hath made us kings and priests unto God and his Father****; to him be glory and dominion for ever and ever. Amen* (Revelation 1:5-6, emphasis mine).

> *But you are a chosen generation, a* ***royal priesthood, a holy nation*** (I Peter 2:9, NKJV, emphasis mine).

Jesus took our unrighteousness and clothed us with His righteousness. "For He made Him who knew no sin to be sin for us, that we might become the righteousness of God in Him" (II Corinthians 5:21, NKJV).

The cross gives us victory over unrighteousness. May the revelation of these truths allow us to walk in the fullness of the power that has been awarded to us by Calvary. And may the weight of our obligation to His great sacrifice keep us in holiness forever. Amen.

Chapter Eight

Victory over Separation

Behold, the LORD'S hand is not so short that it cannot save; nor is His ear so dull that it cannot hear. But your iniquities have made a separation between you and your God, and your sins have hidden His face from you so that He does not hear (Isaiah 59:1-2, NASB).

At the cross Jesus gave us victory over that wall of separation. This wall was created at the fall of man in the Garden of Eden. Adam experienced spiritual death, and a connection was lost. This would leave humanity with a God-shaped void within our spirit, an emptiness we long to fill, but nothing but God can fit in its place. Men have searched the depths of the earth for the substance to fill the emptiness, but it is not there. He digs for gold and mines the silver and cannot find what satisfies this hunger. We think that if we can reach the moon, there we will find satisfaction. We travel to places in the ocean that no eye has ever seen, no bird has looked upon, but it does not exist there either. Job 28 declares what we are looking for we call wisdom, but it is really "the fear of the LORD."

The connection that was lost in the garden was found again in Acts 2 at Pentecost.

> *And when the day of Pentecost was fully come, they were all with one accord in one place. And suddenly there came a sound from heaven as of a rushing mighty wind, and it filled all the house where they were sitting. And there appeared unto them cloven tongues like as of fire, and it sat upon each of them. And they were all filled with the Holy Ghost, and began to speak with other tongues, as the Spirit gave them utterance* (Acts 2:1-4).

The Spirit of the living God was once again breathed into the nostrils of those in the upper room. The church became a "living soul." True life was given, and the same Spirit that raised Christ from the dead was placed inside the hearts of these men and women. This was the church being born into a new race of people. The holy God reunited with His bride. But we must never forget what it took for God to re-establish this lost connection and break down the walls of separation. There could not be a Pentecost without the cross.

Jesus Was Our Intercessor/mediator

> *And at the ninth hour Jesus cried with a loud voice, saying, Eloi, Eloi, lama sabachthani? which is, being interpreted, My God, my God, why hast thou forsaken me?* (Mark 15:34).

The cross was ours to bear, but Jesus took it upon Himself. The trial was ours to stand, yet Jesus stood trial instead of us. Jesus took our place at the whipping post; every thrash that He was struck with should have been on our backs. Every scream, every gasp was ours, but He screamed for us and breathed death's gasping breaths instead of you and me.

He felt the pain that should have been ours. I know we have been covering this point for many chapters now. And as promised, we will drive this point home for the rest of our study of the cross.

Jesus became a sinner and suffered every way that a fallen man suffers (Hebrews 9:28; Matthew 8:17; Isaiah 53:4-6, 11; Psalm 38:4; I Peter 2:24). "For Christ also hath once suffered for sins, the just for the unjust, that he might bring us to God, being put to death in the flesh, but quickened by the Spirit" (I Peter 3:18). Jesus died once and for all. The Righteous died for the unrighteous, the Just for the unjust, the Innocent for the guilty, that Jesus might tear down the walls of separation between us and God. Note how Peter put this next part; Jesus accomplished this by being put to death while He was in a human body. Jesus became our intercessor, someone who intervenes on behalf of someone else.

Jesus interceded for Barabbas, who was sentenced to death along with the two thieves on the day of Calvary. But Jesus took his place. He literally hung on the condemned man's cross. But isn't Barabbas representing the crowd that cried out, "Crucify Him"? or even the entire human race?

While Jesus was on the cross, He called, "My God, my God, why have you forsaken me?" Many people have had trouble understanding this portion of Scripture, especially those who are trying to understand the oneness of God. They may wonder: if Jesus is God, how can He forsake Himself? Or who was Jesus praying to if He is God in the flesh? There are many books written to explain the biblical definition of the Godhead, so I will not venture off into that study. I will, however, focus on this subject as it relates to the cross.

David Bernard gives a clear explanation.

The Dual Nature of Christ

From the Bible we see that Jesus Christ had

two distinct natures in a way that no other human being has ever had. One nature is human or fleshly; the other nature is divine or Spirit. Jesus was both fully man and fully God. The name Jesus refers to the eternal Spirit of God (the Father) dwelling in the flesh. We can use the name Jesus when describing either aspect or both. For example, when we say Jesus died on the cross, we mean His flesh died on the cross. When we say Jesus lives in our hearts, we mean His Spirit is there. We can resolve most questions about the Godhead if we properly understand the dual nature of Jesus. When we read a statement in Scripture about Jesus we should determine whether it describes His deity, His humanity, or both. Moreover, whenever Jesus speaks in Scripture we must determine whether He is speaking from His position as a human, as God, or both. We should not think of two persons in the Godhead or of two Gods, but we should think of the divine Spirit and authentic human flesh. In every way that we humans can speak of our humanity and our relationship to God, so could Jesus, except for sin. Yet He could also speak and act as God. For example, He could sleep one minute and calm the storm the next minute. He could speak as a human and then as God, while being both simultaneously. We must always remember that Jesus is fully God and not merely an anointed man. At the same time, He was fully human, not having just an appearance of humanity. He had a dual nature unlike

> anything we have, and we cannot adequately compare our existence or experience to His. What would seem strange or impossible if applied to a mere human becomes understandable when viewed in the context of One who is both fully God and fully human at the same time.[14]

So as we speak of Jesus on the cross and His death, we are speaking of His human nature. The "man" Christ Jesus is our mediator between God and man (I Timothy 2:5). So as Jesus called out from the cross, "My God, my God, why have you forsaken me?" He was not speaking from His divine nature but crying out as a man who suffered the full weight of the penalty for becoming a sinful man. "God sending his own Son in the likeness of sinful flesh, and for sin, condemned sin in the flesh" (Romans 8:3). Because sinful man had become separated from the Spirit of God, Jesus too had to suffer this separation.

See Daniel Segraves's notes on Hebrews 10.

> We should not think that the sacrifice of Jesus Christ on the cross involved only His physical body. In Hebrew thought, man is integrated so completely that to speak of one part of his existence is to speak of the whole. (See comments on 4:12.) In Isaiah 53:10, the "soul" of the Messiah is an offering for sin. As represented by His body, the entire human

---

[14] *The Oneness of God*, David K. Bernard. Copyright © 1983, 2000 by David K. Bernard Printing history: 1983, 1984, 1985, 1986, 1987, 1989, 1990, 1991, 1992, 1993, 1994, 1995, 1997, 1998, 1999. Revised edition: 2000; pp. 86-88.

> existence of the Messiah was involved in the Atonement. Since this is true, humans are completely redeemed. If only the body of the Messiah had been involved in redemption, presumably only the bodies of people would have been redeemed. But since the Fall in the Garden of Eden resulted in the corruption of not only the material but also the immaterial component of human existence, it was necessary that the Messiah's material and immaterial existence be involved in the redemptive act. His suffering was not limited to His physical body; it extended to His soul and spirit.[15]

These words muttered by Jesus on the cross mark the climax of suffering. Here He drank to the dregs the cup of sorrow, grief, and pain on our behalf. In these hours when the sun refused to shine, Jesus was feeling the full weight of sin. The foreknowledge of God foresaw this day and, through the prophet David, described for us what Jesus felt and thought at this moment.

> *My God, my God, why have you forsaken me? Why are you so far from saving me, so far from my cries of anguish? My God, I cry out by day, but you do not answer, by night, but I find no rest. Yet you are enthroned as the Holy One; you are the one Israel praises. In you our ancestors put their trust; they trusted and you delivered them. To you they cried out and were saved; in you they trusted and were not put to shame. But I am a worm and not a*

---

[15] Segraves, *Hebrews*; chapter 1.

man, scorned by everyone, despised by the people. All who see me mock me; they hurl insults, shaking their heads. "He trusts in the LORD," they say, "let the LORD rescue him. Let him deliver him, since he delights in him" (Psalm 22:1-8, NIV).

Sin Separated Us from God

Here Jesus prayed the prayer of lost humanity. A wall of separation had been constructed by our sin, and we cried from the Fall, "Why have You left us?" The words of Jesus echoed the words from Adam hidden in the bushes. Jesus' cry was real; He was not a robot going through the motions. He felt the bitterness of separation, just as every man has. "For in that He Himself has suffered, being tempted, He is able to aid those who are tempted" (Hebrews 2:18, NKJV). "For we have not an high priest which cannot be touched with the feeling of our infirmities; but was in all points tempted like as we are, yet without sin" (Hebrews 4:15).

The cry from Calvary is often connected to Psalm 22, for obvious reasons. It is not often connected to Isaiah 59, but here we find a prophetic word that will really begin to illuminate the purpose behind the suffering of the cross.

> *Behold, the LORD'S hand is not shortened, that it cannot save; nor His ear heavy, that it cannot hear. But* ***your iniquities have separated you from your God; and your sins have hidden His face from you, so that He will not hear****. For your hands are defiled with blood, and your fingers with iniquity; your lips have spoken lies, your tongue has muttered perversity* (emphasis mine).

Isaiah here has answered the question of fallen, sinful humanity. The question is born from the walls of separation. Our lost cry has been: "My God, why have You forsaken us? Is Your power weakened that You cannot save us [hand shortened]? Have You gone deaf that You cannot hear our cry?" We know that this is the question because Isaiah, through the inspiration of God, here gave us the answer. He explained it is not God's power or His ears that are the problem, but your sins have separated you from God.

Imagine, if you will, you are nailed to your cross. You are paying the penalty for your sins, and the prophet Isaiah walks up. He hears you cry out in your anguish, "My God, why have You forsaken me?" Isaiah then begins to answer your question. "Your hands are defiled with blood, and your lips have spoken lies. You have muttered perversity."

Isaiah goes on as he points his finger into your chest:

> *No one calls for justice, nor does any plead for truth. They trust in empty words and speak lies; they conceive evil and bring forth iniquity.*

You have no honest case for yourself. You're guilty as charged. You trusted in schemes and trickery to get you out of trouble instead of trusting in God.

> *They hatch vipers' eggs. . . .*

Instead of crushing the eggs of the venomous viper, you nurtured them, helping give birth to a breed of deadly snakes.

> *. . . and weave the spider's web; he who eats of their eggs dies, and from that which is crushed a viper breaks out.*

When your plans of evil finally hatch, the true nature of your heart is exposed and a demonic, wicked serpent is born. The venom that runs through your veins only produces more serpents.

> *Their webs will not become garments, nor will they cover themselves with their works;*

Make no mistake, you cannot use these sinful acts to cover your iniquities.

> *Their works are works of iniquity, and the act of violence is in their hands. Their feet run to evil, and they make haste to shed innocent blood; their thoughts are thoughts of iniquity; wasting and destruction are in their paths. The way of peace they have not known, and there is no justice in their ways; they have made themselves crooked paths; whoever takes that way shall not know peace.*

The way of peace mankind has not known because our path is crooked. This is why Jesus had to come "to give light to them that sit in darkness and in the shadow of death, to guide our feet into the way of peace" (Luke 1:79). We need light because we grope in darkness. The darkness is spiritual, caused by our sin.

> *Therefore justice is far from us, nor does righteousness overtake us; we look for light, but there is darkness! for brightness, but we walk in blackness! We grope for the wall like the blind, and we grope as if we had no eyes; we stumble at noonday as at twilight;*

We look for help in God, but He has left us.

> *We are as dead men in desolate places. We all growl like bears, and moan sadly like doves; we look for justice, but there is none; for salvation, but it is far from us. For our transgressions are multiplied before You, and our sins testify against us; for our transgressions are with us, and as for our iniquities, we know them: in transgressing and lying against the LORD, and departing from our God, speaking oppression and revolt, conceiving and uttering from the heart words of falsehood. Justice is turned back, and righteousness stands afar off; for truth is fallen in the street, and equity cannot enter. So truth fails, and he who departs from evil makes himself a prey.*

Isaiah's message brings us no hope whatsoever. We are simply lost in darkness, hanging on our cross to die. What Isaiah just told us, describing our sinful state, are the writings on the documents that are contrary to us (Colossians 2:14). We groaned loud and long. Our words echoed through the ages and into eternity, "My God, my God, why have you forsaken us?" The answer? Nothing.

Our voice could not reach heaven because of our sins. The great wall of separation was too tall, too wide. Our cries could not penetrate it to reach Him. But then . . . just when we think there is no hope . . . Isaiah turns and says:

> *Then the LORD saw it, and it displeased Him that there was no justice. He saw that there was no man, and wondered that there was no intercessor;*

The Lord saw this calamity. He saw that there was no man in heaven nor in the earth who could intercede for us (Revelation 5:2-5). There was no man who could pray our prayer and reach heaven. No one could redeem us, and no one had the ability to atone for our sin.

> *Therefore His own arm brought salvation for Him; and His own righteousness, it sustained Him* (Isaiah 59:1-16, NKJV).

Therefore, God robed Himself in flesh to take on the sins of fallen humanity. He drank the cup of bitterness to the dregs. He became the only man who could pray the prayer of separation that God would actually hear, answer, and bring salvation through. "The LORD is far from the wicked: but he heareth the prayer of the righteous" (Proverbs 15:29). God's own righteousness would save Him (Jesus). "For You will not leave my soul in Sheol, nor will You allow Your Holy One to see corruption" (Psalm 16:10, NKJV).

I don't believe that Isaiah was suggesting that God could not hear man's prayers. Obviously, God spoke to us and we spoke to Him throughout history. What Isaiah was saying is this; there was no way for us to be saved from our lost state. Our wails could not deliver us. There was no person who could become a mediator for the fallen man until Jesus became our ambassador to death.

When Jesus cried out, "My God, my God, why have you forsaken me?" He took our hopeless prayer of desperation and separation and nailed it to the cross. Jesus felt the way we felt, for He became separated from the Spirit of God as He took on the sin of mankind. At the cross, the prayer of fallen humanity was swallowed up in victory. And we now have an advocate with the Father. We now have access through the second Adam.

The Last Adam

> *And the LORD God caused a deep sleep to fall upon Adam, and he slept: and he took one of his ribs, and closed up the flesh instead thereof; and the rib, which the LORD God had taken from man, made he a woman, and brought her unto the man. And Adam said, This is now bone of my bones, and flesh of my flesh: she shall be called Woman, because she was taken out of Man* (Genesis 2:21-23).

The passage of Scripture found here is prophetic illustration of the relationship between God and His bride, the church. God had created the heavens and the earth. The angels were created by Him. The worlds were framed by His hand. Yet if you span the distance of the universe, or eternity for that matter, there is none like God. None can relate to God's character. Our Creator is more than a celestial spirit that covers time and space. God has emotions. He can love, and He can hate. He can be angry, and He can weep. He is a jealous God and a forgiving God. We also know that God feels loneliness or at least understands loneliness, for it was the first emotion God identified in Scripture as "not good." "The LORD God said, 'It is not good for the man to be alone. I will make a helper suitable for him' " (Genesis 2:18, NIV).

It must have pleased the Lord to create man in His image and in His likeness. God created Adam and gave him a world to dominate. Everything Adam could see belonged under his rule. God even allowed Adam to name all of the creatures of the earth, giving ownership to the one who named them. I wonder if Adam looked around all of his world and said to God, "I see the lion and the eagle, Lord, but I do not see one who is like me. I am alone here with no one to relate to; there is no one I can share my life with." I believe when God said, "it is not good for man to be alone," He could relate to the feelings of Adam's loneliness.

I wonder if at this moment God could say, "Now, Adam, you know what it's like to be like Me. I have dominion and rule over My whole world (the universe). Everything is made by Me and belongs to Me, yet there is none like Me. You can now relate to My loneliness and My longing for companionship." Scripture does not give us the fine details of what brought God to the conclusion that it was not good for man to be alone, but I do not think I could be too far off the mark with my imagination here.

So then God caused Adam to fall into a great sleep. And from Adam's side, a bride was formed. She would be bone of his bone and flesh of his flesh. God made a woman to be a companion for Adam. They were joined together as one person for life. In the Garden of Eden these two bonded and fell in love. Heaven only knows the kind of perfect relationship this first couple of the human race experienced while living in the Garden of Eden. The Bible does not give us the time frame for how long their marriage lasted before the Fall. We can only imagine, or maybe not, the perfect love the two shared in a sinless, innocent world.

Then entered Satan, cloaked in the body of the serpent. He tempted Eve, and she fell into his trap of lies. Genesis 3 lines out the details of this tragic event. We know that Eve was deceived by the devil. She actually believed the fruit of the forbidden tree was good to eat. She did not know that she would die. "And Adam was not deceived, but the woman being deceived, fell into transgression" (I Timothy 2:14, NKJV). Eve ate from the tree and instantly lost her spiritual covering. Her death occurred before Adam's. Adam was not deceived. In other words, Adam knew full well that when he sinned, he would suffer the same consequences as his bride

Eve. He knew he would die, but he also knew he was now separated from Eve. Just as Eve became separated from God, I believe there was a separation between Adam and his wife.

So Adam took on the sin of his bride in order to restore their relationship connection. As romantic as that may sound, this decision caused Adam to be separated from God. The bliss once shared by God and His creation was lost. It is "not good" that God should be alone.

That was the first Adam. And then God did something that not even the angels understand (I Peter 1:12). God took on the form of fallen humanity. In order to restore our lost connection, God had to become a second Adam (I Corinthians 15:45). This last Adam did what the first Adam did in the Garden of Eden. He took on the sin of His bride in order to save the lost connection. The last Adam had to become like her in order to save her. Jesus ate of the tree knowing full well that it would cause Him to lose His connection with the Father. Jesus knew full well that by taking on her sin, He would surely suffer and would surely die.

And so here we find our last Adam, hanging lifeless upon the tree. Jesus took upon Himself the curse from the garden, His bride scattered around His feet, lost in her sin. "Forgive My bride, Father; she is lost in sin. She does not understand what she has done. Forgive them; for they know not what they do" (Luke 23:34). Jesus interceded for the love of His life and then uttered the final words of His life, His mission and His purpose: "It is finished."

Jesus hung between heaven and earth, no breath left in Him. His heart had completed its last beat. The Roman soldier approached the last Adam and drove a spear through His side and pierced His heart. As blood and water flowed, God formed a bride from the bleeding side of Jesus. Just like Eve was formed from the first Adam, so was the church formed from the last Adam, out of His side.

Adam had fallen into a great sleep when Eve was taken out of his side. Likewise, Jesus had entered into His great sleep (death) for just a little while (John 11:11). Then when Jesus awoke . . . the work had been done. The walls of separation had fallen. The bride of Christ was formed. "For we are members of his body, of his flesh, and of his bones" (Ephesians 5:30). Jesus then told His disciples to go to Jerusalem and wait for the promise of the Holy Ghost. The pathway had been opened, and now God has full communion with His long-lost bride.

God breathed life back into us through the baptism of the Holy Spirit. That God-shaped hole within us is full and is totally satisfied. We can now pray in the Spirit; we can intercede for the lost. The church has become the companion of Christ. We have taken on His nature and His character. His mind dwells in our mind. His way is our way. He has lighted our pathway and shown us the lifestyle of peace. There is no greater moment in all of our eternal existence that will compare to the time when Jesus called our name from the cross and wrapped us in the loving arms of mercy and grace. This is why I will always cling to that old rugged cross.

On a hill far away, stood an old rugged cross,
The emblem of suff'ring and shame;
And I love that old cross, where the dearest and best
For a world of lost sinners was slain.

So I'll cherish the old rugged cross,
Till my trophies at last I lay down;
I will cling to the old rugged cross,
And exchange it some day for a crown.

O that old rugged cross, so despised by the world,
Has a wondrous attraction for me;

For the dear Lamb of God left his Glory above
To bear it to dark Calvary.

In the old rugged cross, stained with blood so divine,
A wondrous beauty I see;
For 'twas on that old cross, Jesus suffered and died
To pardon and sanctify me.

To the old rugged cross I will ever be true,
Its shame and reproach gladly bear;
Then he'll call me some day to my home far away,
Where his glory forever I'll share.

So I'll cherish the old rugged cross,
Till my trophies at last I lay down;
I will cling to the old rugged cross,
And exchange it some day for a crown.[16]

---

[16]"The Old Rugged Cross," words and music by George Bennard. Public domain.

Chapter Nine

The Piercings

> *Christ hath redeemed us from the curse of the law, being made a curse for us: for it is written, Cursed is every one that hangeth on a tree* (Galatians 3:13).

As noted in the earlier chapter, the form of death was crucial for God to accomplish total freedom and deliverance for lost humanity. Nothing was done by accident. The details of the execution play an important role in our redemption. Looking again at Colossians, we see that Jesus abolished the documents against us by nailing them to His cross.

> *Blotting out the handwriting of ordinances that was against us, which was contrary to us, and took it out of the way,* ***nailing it to his cross*** (Colossians 2:14, emphasis mine).

We will focus on this detail for the next two chapters, which deal with the piercings of Christ. The piercings were in the plan of God from the very beginning. Long before crucifixion was even invented, God had already planned it out. Death penalty by the Jews was always carried out by stoning. The Romans, however, had developed the cross as a cruel form of execution. So by the providence of God, Jesus would come to die while the Jews had no power to stone Him and the Romans had all power to crucify Him, for the nails served as an important role in our redemption. See the following verses of Scripture (emphases mine throughout).

> *For dogs have compassed me: the assembly of the wicked have inclosed me: they* ***pierced my hands and my feet*** (Psalm 22:16).

> *And they shall look upon me* ***whom they have pierced****, and they shall mourn for him, as one mourneth for his only son, and shall be in bitterness for him, as one that is in bitterness for his firstborn* (Zechariah 12:10b).

> *For these things were done, that the scripture should be fulfilled, A bone of him shall not be broken. And again another scripture saith, They shall look on* ***him whom they pierced*** (John 19:36-37).

The piercings are what was literally "nailed to His cross." Colossians 2:14 indicates that by the nails Jesus abolished the documents and rendered them useless. Jesus suffered three piercings; His hands, His feet, and then His side were pierced. We will examine each of these separately.

Hands

We will not rehearse again the Scriptures that show how Jesus took our place on the cross. I believe that point has been well made. However, we must keep this in the forefront of our minds as we study the cross.

The use of the word "hands" plays a special role in Scripture. The word "hand" is found over eighteen hundred times in the English Bible. One-third of these describes the hand as the physical body part at the end of the arm. It's what man uses to take possession of items. A man's craftwork is called "the works of his hands" (Deuteronomy 28:12). We use our hands for greeting others and also in forms of worship, as clapping and lifting our hands.

The other two-thirds of the use of the term "hands" refer to figurative or metaphoric references. God refers to the hand as power and strength. Moses told the children of Israel that they should not think that the power of their own hands would give them prosperity (Deuteronomy 8:17). Throughout the Scriptures God used the term "hand" to illustrate His own power and ability as well.

The hand is used also to define authority, possession, and control. "And the hand of the children of Israel grew stronger and stronger against Jabin king of Canaan" (Judges 4:24a, NKJV). The Lord had delivered the enemy into the hands of Israel. "Hands" here is not literal but indicative of authority, power, and control.

The "right hand" is also used to denote total power and position. To be seated on the "right hand of the throne" would be understood that the right hand was the position of the king himself.

Hands are used as an idiom for consecration and dedication. The term "laying on of the hands" is used numerous times. The priests laid their hands upon sacrifices for atonement. We lay hands on the sick, and God's power heals them.

While the hand is a body part at the end of the arm, it is much more than this in biblical imagery. Whether in performing tasks, expressing power and authority, or designating purpose and function, the hand is a pervasive picture reflecting the wishes and will of the entire person.

Remember Isaiah 59 from the previous chapter? Here Isaiah answered the question asked by lost humanity, "Why have You forsaken us?" The prophet detailed our sinful status and revealed the cause of our separation from God. He explained that it was not God's fault that we are lost and without hope, but rather our iniquity has built this barrier:

> *Behold, the LORD'S hand is not shortened, that it cannot save; neither his ear heavy, that it cannot hear: but your iniquities have separated between you and your God, and your sins have hid his face from you, that he will not hear.* ***For your hands are defiled with blood, and your fingers with iniquity****; your lips have spoken lies, your tongue hath muttered perverseness. None calleth for justice, nor any pleadeth for truth: they trust in vanity, and speak lies; they conceive mischief, and bring forth iniquity. They hatch cockatrice' eggs, and weave the spider's web: he that eateth of their eggs dieth, and that which is crushed breaketh out into a viper. Their webs shall not become garments, neither shall they cover themselves with their works: their works are works of iniquity,* ***and the act of violence is in their hands*** (Isaiah 59:1-7, emphases mine).

God described our fallen state by using the hands as a metaphor for our acts of sin. In the eyes of God, our sins are like bloody hands. Isaiah told us that we are guilty of murder, for our hands are bloody. This is referring to the shedding of innocent blood. Our hands have been rendered unholy, for we have touched the unclean things. Our fingers have caressed the forbidden fruits of sinful lusts. Notice Isaiah declared that the problem is not in God's hand (His power) but the problem is with our hands (verses 1, 3). It is not that we have all committed murder, but all of us have "bloody hands" because of our sinful nature. We are all guilty of being sinners, and our hands are stained with sin.

Our hands are defiled; therefore, we have lost our dominion and authority. Figuratively, we have no power or strength. Our defiled hands, figuratively, represent one-third of our sinful nature. Thus, Jesus took upon Himself our bloody hands and literally nailed them to His cross. The other two-thirds are our feet and heart.

When the Romans drove the nails in the wrists, pinning the arms and hands to the cross, they pierced the median nerve. This pain was so intense a word was needed that could somehow describe this pain. They came up the word "excruciating," or "out of the cross." It has been noted that those who experience similar wounds to the median nerve often consider suicide as a means to end their misery. The pierced hands and feet became the agony of the cross. This was the greatest physical pain endured during the crucifixion. Jesus did this so that our hands could be clean.

As we are washed in the blood of the Lamb and we are born again, we regain our authority and dominion (Ephesians 1:21). Our clean hands give us a position with God. We are made to be a royal priesthood, a holy nation (I Peter 2:9). Power and authority are granted to us as we will judge with God (I Corinthians 6:2; Luke 22:29-30).

We have been given power to lay our hands upon the sick, and they shall recover (Mark 16:17-18). Through the laying on of hands, anointing is transferred and our calling is secured in God (I Timothy 4:14). "And by the hands of the apostles were many signs and wonders wrought among the people" (Acts 5:12a). Laying on of the hands is an important doctrine of the church. Hebrews identifies the practice as part of the foundation of the church:

> *Therefore leaving the principles of the doctrine of Christ, let us go on unto perfection; not laying again the foundation of repentance from dead works, and of faith toward God, of the doctrine of baptisms, and of laying on of hands, and of resurrection of the dead, and of eternal judgment* (Hebrews 6:1-2).

This is more than just a mere act; this refers to the presence and the power of the Holy Spirit working within the new body of Jesus Christ, the church. See David K. Bernard's notes.

> Purpose and Significance
> of Laying on of the Hands
>
> *First*, the laying on of hands *symbolizes the transfer of blessings from God to us.* This practice is particularly helpful in praying for (1) blessing, (2) healing, (3) reception of the Holy Spirit, and (4) ordination to and anointing for service.
>
> *Second*, the practice *signifies the joint work of God's Spirit and God's church* to bring these blessings to individuals. While God is sovereign and can perform these works without human hands, He wants to move through His church. While the blessings come from God, the church proclaims them and inspires people to have faith to receive them.
>
> *Third*, it *represents submission to God and His church.* In everyday life, touching another person's head expresses intimacy or authority.

> A typical example is when an adult pats a child on the head. It is rare for one adult to touch another adult's head in public. When we allow elders to lay hands on our head in prayer, we demonstrate our submission to God and to godly leaders. Prayer by itself acknowledges our need of God, but prayer with the laying on of hands acknowledges our need for both God and the church. Moreover, since the Bible teaches the laying on of hands, our acceptance of it is an act of obedient faith.
>
> *Fourth*, the practice *represents consecration to God.* Humble submission over time leads to consecrated service. When those who seek the Holy Spirit receive the laying on of hands, they express not only their desire to receive the Spirit but also their new dedication to God. At an ordination service, the recipients not only seek the blessing and anointing of God upon their lives but they also signify their consecration to Him and His church.
>
> *Fifth*, the laying on of hands is a powerful tool that *focuses people's faith to receive a promise from God at a particular time.*[17]

Jesus took our position of impotence and nailed it to the cross, thereby granting to the church a position of power and a place of authority. The action of the spiritual gifts operating in the church can be categorized into three manifestations: the mind of Christ, the hands of Christ, and the voice of Christ (I Corinthians 12). Some summarize this teaching by

---

[17] *Spiritual Gifts*, David K. Bernard. ©1997 David K. Bernard, Hazelwood, MO 63042-2299; pp. 178-179.

saying "we are the hands and the feet of Christ." We have become the hands of Christ in power and authority because Jesus took care of our sinful hands at the cross.

The point that I am trying to resolve here is that all of the power and authority given to the church is the hand of God or the power of God in action through us. God has instructed us literally to use our hands to invoke the power and authority from heaven to earth.

When we lay hands on someone or something, we are bringing two worlds together. The only way this could ever be possible is if we have "clean hands." The next time you lay hands on someone for him to receive anything from God, just remember the nails. You are invoking the power of the cross on behalf of the person you are praying for. There is a transfer of power and authority that stems from Calvary. Scripture tells us that by His stripes we are healed, and we are commissioned to pray for healing by laying our hands upon those with illnesses, thus bringing the cross into the realm of the present need.

Feet

> *Their webs shall not become garments, neither shall they cover themselves with their works: their works are works of iniquity, and the act of violence is in their hands.* ***Their feet run to evil,*** *and they make haste to shed innocent blood: their thoughts are thoughts of iniquity; wasting and destruction are in their paths.* ***The way of peace they know not****; and there is no judgment in their goings:* ***they have made them crooked paths****: whosoever goeth therein shall not know peace* (Isaiah 59:6-8, emphases mine).

Like the hands, feet are used figuratively throughout the Bible. Our feet can give us rights to ownership where our feet may stand, as in Psalm 122:2 (NKJV): "Our feet have been standing within your gates, O Jerusalem!" Having one's feet over something is a sign of dominion, similar to the hands. Jesus' feet will stand on Mt. Olivet, and Satan will be crushed under His feet (Genesis 3:15).

Feet are also symbolic of one's ability to stand in righteousness. "The LORD God is my strength; He will make my feet like deer's feet, and He will make me walk on my high hills" (Habakkuk 3:19, NKJV). And this example: "Uphold my steps in Your paths, that my footsteps may not slip" (Psalm 17:5, NKJV).

Our feet, in the eyes of God, are associated with our lifestyle, or "the way we take." When David said that the Word of God is a lamp unto my feet and a light unto my path (Psalm 119:105), he was not referring to the Word lighting up literal darkness so he could navigate the path. He was, however, saying that the Word of God can guide his lifestyle in the ways of righteousness.

Isaiah clearly let us know that our feet are on the wrong paths. Because of our sinful nature, the very path of our feet is wickedness. He told us that our feet run to evil. The graphic description he used illustrates this point.

> *They hatch the eggs of vipers and spin a spider's web. Whoever eats their eggs will die, and when one is broken, an adder is hatched. Their cobwebs are useless for clothing; they cannot cover themselves with what they make. Their deeds are evil deeds, and acts of violence are in their hands. Their feet rush into sin; they are swift to shed innocent blood* (Isaiah 59:5-7, NIV).

Our way of life is filled with lies, injustice, conniving, and stealing, and every plan we devise ends in the death of the innocent. Our "way" does not know God nor does it lead us to peace. Our paths are not straight (righteous), but our feet run and choose the wicked, crooked paths.

> *These six things doth the LORD hate: yea, seven are an abomination unto him: A proud look, a lying tongue, and hands that shed innocent blood, an heart that deviseth wicked imaginations,* ***feet that be swift in running to mischief,*** *a false witness that speaketh lies, and he that soweth discord among brethren* (Proverbs 6:16-19, emphasis mine).

Jesus came to the darkness, stepping into our crooked paths in order to bring light. "To give light to them that sit in darkness and in the shadow of death, to guide our feet into the way of peace" (Luke 1:79). Jesus accomplished this victory for us by taking our feet to Calvary and nailing them to His cross. If our hands represent one-third of our sinful state, then our feet are another one-third.

Another moment of extreme pain was experienced through this torturous event, but it was all in the plan of God. Our wicked feet were swallowed up in victory, and now we can walk a straight path. Everything we stand on we have dominion over. The gates of hell cannot prevail against the church (Matthew 16:18). "And the God of peace shall bruise Satan under your feet shortly. The grace of our Lord Jesus Christ be with you" (Romans 16:20). Our way of life now centers on the kingdom of God. Our kingdom has fallen and our old paths are abolished. The race we run is that of glory. The gospel message has been placed within our care because our feet have been made beautiful by the blood of Jesus.

> *And how shall they preach, except they be sent? as it is written, How beautiful are the feet of them that preach the gospel of peace, and bring glad tidings of good things!* (Romans 10:15).

When Jesus began to wash the disciples' feet at the Last Supper, much more was happening than may have met the eye. What Jesus did there in the physical, He was about to do in the spiritual. If we do not allow our feet to be cleansed by Jesus, we will have no part in Him. If we do not accept the new paths and the righteous standing, we will not know Him or the way of peace.

> *Peter saith unto him, Thou shalt never wash my feet. Jesus answered him, If I wash thee not, thou hast no part with me. Simon Peter saith unto him, Lord, not* ***my feet*** *only, but also* ***my hands*** *and* ***my head*** (John 13:8-9, emphases mine).

What a powerful statement made by the disciple! Peter was expressing his desire for Jesus to wash him wholly and completely. Wash my feet, my hands, and my head. Again, notice Peter's description of a complete man is one-third hands, one-third feet, and one-third head (or mind, heart). All three piercings were mentioned. And that is exactly what Jesus did on the cross. He took our complete sinful man and nailed him to the cross.

Heart

> *But when they came to Jesus, and saw that he was dead already, they brake not his legs: but*

> *one of the soldiers with a* **spear pierced his side**, *and forthwith came there out blood and water. And he that saw it bare record, and his record is true: and he knoweth that he saith true, that ye might believe. For these things were done, that the scripture should be fulfilled, A bone of him shall not be broken* (John 19:33-36, emphasis mine).

It was not common for a man being crucified to be riven with a spear. The standard practice was to break the leg bones so that the person being executed would no longer be able to push up with his legs, allowing his diaphragm to take a breath. Thus, the victim would suffocate and expire much faster. This was the Roman soldier's plan, but when he approached Jesus to break His legs, Jesus was already dead. So he ran the spear into His heart.

The details of the cross absolutely, without question, validate Jesus as the Messiah and provide insight as to what was accomplished for us on that fateful day. When God told Moses to prepare for the Passover, he was given explicit instructions not to break any of the bones of the lamb to be sacrificed (Exodus 12:46). John the Baptist introduced Jesus as the "Lamb of God, who takes away the sin of the world" (John 1:29). Jesus fulfilled every detail of the Passover lamb, including having none of His bones broken. "For these things were done, that the scripture should be fulfilled, A bone of him shall not be broken" (John 19:36). The prophecy was found in Psalm 34:20 (NIV): "He protects all his bones, not one of them will be broken."

This was done not only to fulfill prophecy and prove the authority of the Messiah but to complete all the necessary piercings of the sinful man. As the spear was driven into the side of our Lord, blood and water flowed.

Hastings' Dictionary of Christ and the Gospels gives some insight on this phenomenon.

> When the soldier, whom tradition names Longinus, to make sure that He was really dead, drove his spear into the side of Jesus on the cross (see Crucifixion), a strange thing happened. On being withdrawn the spear was followed by a gush of blood and water. It was a singular phenomenon. The Fathers regarded it as a miracle, but St. John does not venture on an opinion. He neither attempts to account for it nor pronounces it a miracle, but contents himself with solemnly asseverating that he had witnessed it, and could vouch for its actual occurrence. He felt the wonder of it to the last (cf. 1 John 5:6-8).
>
> Medical science has confirmed his testimony, and furnished an explanation which at once defines the phenomenon as a perfectly natural occurrence, and reveals somewhat of the awfulness of our Lord's Passion. During His dread and mysterious dereliction on the cross (see Dereliction) His heart swelled until it burst, and the blood was 'effused into the distended sac of the pericardium, and afterwards separated, as is usual with extravasated blood, into these two parts, viz. (1) crassamentum or red clot, and (2) watery serum.' When the distended sac was pierced from beneath, it discharged 'its sanguineous contents in the form of red clots of blood and a stream of watery serum, exactly corresponding to the description given by the sacred

> narrative, "and forthwith came there out blood and water." ' Jesus died literally of a broken heart—of 'agony of mind, producing rupture of the heart.'[18]

Jesus' physical heart was pierced, just like His physical hands and feet. But like the hands and feet, the heart has many metaphoric uses in Scripture.

> **Personality**. The heart is used metaphorically to describe the intangibles that constitute what it means to be human. In this sense it is the antonym of the "flesh" or *body. We see this in the psalmist's confession, "My flesh and my heart may fail, but God is the strength of my heart and my portion forever" (Ps 73:26 NIV). To use a modern idiom, the heart is often used in the Bible to describe "what makes us tick," that is, human personality. In other words, the heart is used to describe those dynamic forces that make us unique individuals. As such, the heart can be imbued with moral qualities. For instance, the poet in Ps 131:1 claims that his "heart is not proud" (cf. 2 Chron 32:26). Hearts can also be "evil" (1 Sam 17:28) or "deluded" (Isa 44:20; cf. Jer 17:9).
>
> **Intellect and Memory**. We associate thought and memory with the brain today, but

---

[18] *Hastings' Dictionary of Christ and the Gospels*, and *Dictionary of the Apostolic Church*. Biblesoft formatted electronic database. Copyright © 2015 by Biblesoft, Inc. All rights reserved.

in the idiom of the Bible, thinking is a function of the heart. The psalmist thought about his present difficult situation in the light of his past. As he "remembered [his] songs in the night," he says, "My heart mused and my spirit inquired" (Ps 77:6 NIV). As a prelude to the *flood, the book of Genesis tells us that God noted "how great man's wickedness on the earth had become, and that every inclination of the thoughts of his heart was only evil all the time" (Gen 6:5 NIV).

Emotions. According to biblical usage, the heart is the source from which the emotions flow. Aaron's heart flows with *joy when he sees Moses (Ex 4:14). Lev 19:17 warns God's people not to hate their brother in their heart. Fear is expressed as a loss of heart (Deut 1:28), indicating that courage is also a heartfelt emotion (Ps 27:3). These and many other emotions—for instance, despair (Deut 28:65), sadness (Neh 2:2), trust (Ps 28:7) and *anger (Ps 39:3)—are said to come from one's heart.

Will. The heart not only thinks and feels, remembers and desires, but it also chooses a course of action. Jesus himself taught that "out of the heart come evil thoughts, *murder, *adultery, *sexual immorality, *theft, false testimony, slander" (Matt 15:19 NIV). The obstinacy of the human heart is also an act of will (Deut 2:30), and here we may mention the many references in the book of Exodus to the "hard heart" of *Pharaoh (e.g., Ex 4:21; 7:3; 8:15). This is a heart that refuses to choose in

> accordance with God's will, which leads ultimately to the Egyptian king's destruction.[19]

Our heart represents our personality, intellect, emotions, and will. Scripture often refers to our soul as the intellect, the mind, or the "heart" of man. The sinner's heart is wicked at best. Left to our own desires, we fall desperately into sinful acts. "The heart is deceitful above all things, and desperately wicked: who can know it?" (Jeremiah 17:9). Remember the six things that God hates—a proud look, a lying tongue, hands that shed innocent blood, a heart that deviseth wicked imaginations, feet are swift in running to mischief, a false witness, and a sower of discord (Proverbs 6:16-19)? God took to this evil heart to His cross, and there it was pierced. Through the power of the cross, God can give us a new heart.

> *Then will I sprinkle clean water upon you, and ye shall be clean: from all your filthiness, and from all your idols, will I cleanse you.* ***A new heart also will I give you****, and a new spirit will I put within you: and I will take away the* ***stony heart out of your flesh,*** *and I will give you an heart of flesh. And I will put my spirit within you,* ***and cause you to walk in my statutes****, and ye shall keep my judgments, and do them. And ye shall dwell in the land that I gave to your fathers; and ye shall be my people, and I will be your God* (Ezekiel 36:25-28, emphases mine).

---

[19] *Dictionary of Biblical Imagery*.

Ezekiel told us that God will wash us with clean water and put a new heart within us. This new heart will cause our feet to walk in the path of righteousness. Our hearts, our hands, and our feet caused us to be separated from God, but now, we can walk boldly into the throne room of grace.

> *Who shall ascend into the hill of the LORD? or who shall stand in his holy place? He that hath clean hands, and a pure heart; who hath not lifted up his soul unto vanity, nor sworn deceitfully* (Psalm 24:3-4).

Who shall stand with his feet in God's holy place? Those who have clean hands and a pure heart. The nails give us access to God's holiness. The nails allow us to become separated unto Him, a holy people.

Why should we live holy? Because of the nails. Why should we be a separated people? Because of the "excruciating" pain that our Lord endured to give us the ability to be cleansed from all sin and to enter into God's holy hill.

Missing the Mark

Our evil heart could never keep the statutes of the law. Whenever we tried to do good, evil was with us. Our hearts were incapable of righteousness; therefore, the mosaic law was not able to keep us from sin. The definition of sin is missing the mark. It was derived from an archer who, when he missed the target, was said to have sinned. So when we miss the mark of God, we are sinning. From the time of Adam to Moses, death reigned and there was no law (Romans 5:13-14). Figuratively, it would be as if man were shooting his arrows, trying to hit a target he could not even see. Hence, death reigned from Adam to Moses.

The mosaic law was written on cold tablets of stone. The law, though it showed us the way of righteousness, could not fix our heart problem. The religious leaders in Jesus' day held fast to the teachings of the law. But as Jesus told them, their hearts were still corrupted. No matter how well anyone followed the book of rules, he was still a sinner at heart.

> *Ye have heard that it was said by them of old time, Thou shalt not kill . . . but I say unto you, That whosoever is angry with his brother without a cause shall be in danger of the judgment* (Matthew 5:21-22a).

You can obey the letter of the law, but your heart has not been changed from its original sinful state. Jesus further explained that if you wash the cup on the outside, the inside is left dirty. "Now do ye Pharisees make clean the outside of the cup and the platter; but your inward part is full of ravening and wickedness" (Luke 11:39). But if we allow Jesus to purify our hearts and wash us from the inside, our outside will be clean as well. With our hearts defiled, all our good deeds become hypocrisy. The Lord needed to write His law inside us, not on tablets of stone but upon hearts of flesh.

When God gave Moses the law, it gave us the target. We could now see what we needed to hit. But because the law could not change our hearts, we still couldn't hit the target. All the law did was show us how far off the mark we were (Romans 3:20). The law could not teach us to become better archers, so it did not fix the problem. (See Hebrews 8 and Romans 7).

But the new covenant gave us both the target and the teacher. If God could somehow change our hearts, cleansing us from the inside out, then He could put His law inside us. And He certainly can do that through the Atonement!

> *"This is the covenant I will make with the house of Israel after that time," declares the LORD. "I will put my law in their minds and write it on their hearts. I will be their God, and they will be my people"* (Jeremiah 31:33, NIV).

The prophet foretold of a time when God would change our hearts. Ezekiel had stated that God would take out the stony heart and give a heart of flesh. The law of Moses was written on stone, but after Calvary, God would write it on our hearts.

His Spirit in us is our teacher who shows us how to hit the mark. Remember that the law was our bond-servant that brought us to our teacher, Christ (Galatians 3:24). The Holy Spirit is the Spirit of our teacher who leads and guides us into all truth. "If we live in the Spirit, let us also walk in the Spirit" (Galatians 5:25). When God puts His Spirit inside us, it changes our heart and therefore changes our walk. Through the crucifixion of Jesus we have been cleansed. When the flesh was torn, our hearts were purified and we were set free.

> *By a new and living way, which he hath consecrated for us, through the veil, that is to say, his flesh; and having an high priest over the house of God; let us draw near with a* ***true heart*** *in full assurance of faith, having our* ***hearts sprinkled from an evil conscience****, and our bodies washed with pure water* (Hebrews 10:20-23, emphases mine).

A Holy Temple

With our hearts purified, our hands cleansed, and our feet on the path of righteousness, we have been washed wholly. Like Peter at the Last Supper, we request, "Not only my feet, Lord. Wash all of me." We have been made pure from head to toe. God has done this not only to save us from death but also to purify a holy temple, a dwelling place for His Spirit. "Know ye not that ye are the ***temple*** of God, and that the Spirit of God dwelleth in you?" (I Corinthians 3:16, emphasis mine).

The temple of the Lord has many parts. The outer court is the location of the burnt offerings. Then there is the inner court, where you will find the table of showbread, the altar of incense, and the seven golden candlesticks. And then there is the Most Holy Place. This is where the mercy seat rests on the ark of the covenant. In this place, behind the veil, the glory of God comes down to consume the blood of sacrifices presented by the high priest of Israel. This is the portal between God's people and God's throne, the place that connects heaven and earth.

When Paul said that we are the temple of the Lord, he was not referring to the outer court nor the inner court. Paul used the Greek *naos*, which denotes that our bodies have become the Most Holy Place within the tabernacle. "But ye are washed, but ye are sanctified, but ye are justified in the name of the Lord Jesus, and by the Spirit of our God" (I Corinthians 6:11b). We have been washed, sanctified, and justified by the name Jesus and by the Spirit of God.

As stated in previous chapters, we become recipients of the power of the cross and every benefit associated with it when we are washed in the watery grave of baptism in the name of Jesus and then are filled with the Holy Spirit of promise (Acts 2:38). Being born again of water and of the Spirit grants us sanctification, justification, and cleansing. We become totally cleansed from head to toe when we are washed in the blood and then filled with His Spirit. I thank God for the pierced body of Jesus Christ.

A Nail in a Sure Place

The inspiration of the prophet Isaiah regarding the coming Messiah is unmatched by any of the other Old Testament prophets. Isaiah is suitably called the Messianic Prophet. In chapter 22 we read about the Messiah, pre-figured in this text as Eliakim the son of Hilkiah being like a nail fastened in a sure place.

> *And I will clothe him with thy robe, and strengthen him with thy girdle, and I will commit thy government into his hand: and he shall be a father to the inhabitants of Jerusalem, and to the house of Judah. [See Isaiah 9:6.] And the key of the house of David will I lay upon his shoulder; so he shall open, and none shall shut; and he shall shut, and none shall open* (Isaiah 22:21-22).

The keys symbolize the authority of the kingdom will be given to Jesus. Of course we know that Jesus was given preeminence over every office, including the keys to death and the grave (Colossians 2:9-15; Revelation 1:18).

> *And I will fasten him as a nail in a sure place; and he shall be for a glorious throne to his father's house. And they shall hang upon him all the glory of his father's house, the offspring and the issue, all vessels of small quantity, from the vessels of cups, even to all the vessels of flagons* (Isaiah 22:23-24).

God took our Savior and fastened Him to a Roman cross. The cross was an instrument of torture, pain, and death. But to

God, the cross of Jesus was a "sure place." The cross became the instrument of our salvation.

Isaiah was using the verbiage here that described a spike driven into a secure place within a person's home. Nails where used to hang useful household objects. If these nails were to hold anything of real value, they needed to be fastened into a place that would be able to hold the weight of everything hanging on them. Jesus became the nail that was driven into a secure place. The cross became our secure salvation, and upon Jesus (our nail fastened to the cross) God will hang all of the treasures of His house. Isaiah used household vessels to describe the diversity of all lost souls. From the gold and silver to the meager vessels of clay and wood, God will hang upon this nail every man, from the least to the greatest, from the poor to the rich. Every soul that lives will be placed upon this nail. Isaiah let us know that this nail will be secure, driven in by God Himself. Friend, the nails that secured Jesus to the cross were God's way of securing our salvation into a sure place.

Jesus told Thomas, "Behold My nail-scarred hands and My riven side." The visible image of the nail prints brought Thomas to His knees. "Then he said to Thomas, 'Put your finger here; see my hands. Reach out your hand and put it into my side. Stop doubting and believe.' Thomas said to him, 'My Lord and my God!' " (John 20:27-28, NIV). Beholding the nail prints made all the difference for Thomas. He then declared Jesus to be Jehovah.

This connection between the nail-scarred hands and Jehovah are linked back to the Hebrew alphabet. The name of God in the Hebrew text is transliterated YHWH. This name of God appears in the Old Testament nearly six thousand times. YHWH is spelled with four letters called the Tetragrammaton. Rev. Don Grigsby, who pastors in a town near me, taught about the Hebrew word for YHWH at a camp meeting in Texas. He explained how each letter of the Hebrew alphabet was derived from pictograms. In other words, each symbol represents a figure of some sort. If you look at the four letters that make up the Tetragrammaton, the name YHWH, you will see a message unfolding in the spelling of the name of Jehovah.

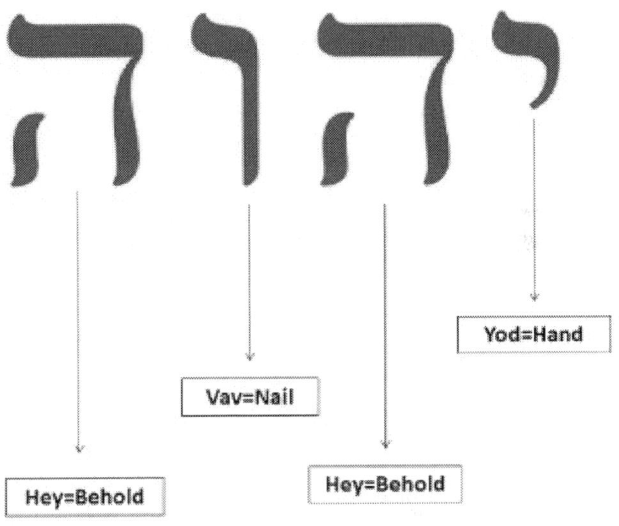

As Hebrew is read right to left, this is spelled YOD, HEY, VAV, HEY. We read it, "Behold, behold the nailed hands." When Jesus spoke these words to Thomas and revealed His hands, Thomas fell before His Yahweh and said, "My Lord and my God" (John 20:28b). The word "Lord" in this text is from the Greek *Kúrios* which is the equivalent for the Old Testament Hebrew Jehovah. And then Thomas added "God" from the Greek *Theøs*, which in the New Testament is the name of the one true God. Jesus became the pictogram or the image of the name that God used nearly six thousand times in the Old Testament.

Consider Adam Clarke's view of this moment.

Those who deny the Godhead of Christ would have us to believe that these words are an exclamation of Thomas, made through surprise, and that they were addressed to the Father and not to Christ. The text is plain: Jesus comes in—sees Thomas and addresses him; desiring him to come to him, and put his finger into the print of the nails, etc. Thomas perfectly satisfied of the reality of our Lord's resurrection, says unto him,—My LORD! and My GOD! i.e. Thou art indeed the very same person,—my Lord whose disciple I have so long been; and thou art my God, henceforth the object of my religious adoration. Thomas was the first who gave the title of God to Jesus; and, by this glorious confession, made some amends for his former obstinate incredulity. It is worthy of remark, that from this time forward the whole of the disciples treated our Lord with the most supreme respect, never using that familiarity toward him which they had often used before. The resurrection from the dead gave them the fullest proof of the divinity of Christ. And this, indeed, is the use which John makes of this manifestation of Christ. See John 20:30-31. Dr. Pearce says here: "Observe that Thomas calls Jesus his God, and that Jesus does not reprove him for it, though probably it was the first time he was called so." And, I would ask, could Jesus be jealous of the honour of the true God—could he be a prophet—could he be even an honest

> man, to permit his disciple to indulge in a mistake so monstrous and destructive, if it had been one?[20]

The nails at the cross give the proof that Jesus is the Messiah and Jehovah all in one. Jesus has become the image of the invisible God, the glory of God manifested in the flesh (Colossians 1:15; I Timothy 3:16). By His own hand He brought salvation to us all. What an incredible revelation this must have been for Thomas! And Jesus responded to this great revelation by saying: "Thomas, because thou hast seen me, thou hast believed: blessed are they that have not seen, and yet have believed" (John 20:29).

We are a blessed people to have this same great revelation about the Messiah although we have not beheld the nail-scarred hands. He has come to set the captives free, to heal the brokenhearted, to robe us with righteousness, to redeem us from sin, and to give us a place of dominion and power. We will reign with Him in glory for ever and ever.

---

[20]Clarke, *Adam Clarke's Commentary.*

Chapter Ten

The Crown of Thorns

And they stripped Him and put a scarlet robe on Him. When they had twisted a crown of thorns, they put it on His head, and a reed in His right hand. And they bowed the knee before Him and mocked Him, saying, "Hail, King of the Jews!" (Matthew 27:28-29, NKJV).

We have already discussed the robes that were placed on Jesus and the victory won for us through this mockery. However, I have left the significance of the crown of thorns for its own study. The rabbinical books mention no less than twenty-two words in the Bible signifying thorny plants, and the word *akantha* used in Matthew 27 is generic and not specific to any particular plant. I have read several places that the thorns used for the crown were one to two inches in length, and the Roman soldiers had to use a hammer to drive them into His skull. Yet other sources indicate the plant was thin and the thorns were very small.

I do not feel that the length of the thorns or the type of plant used is critical. Otherwise, those facts would have been stated in Scripture. The significance lies in the fact that it was most certainly a thorn bush.

Thorns

Scripture mentions thorns many times throughout its pages. Like the hand, heart, and feet, the term "thorns" is used many times metaphorically to denote negativity. The *Dictionary of Biblical Imagery* gives examples.

> In two dozen books of the OT and NT, thorn imagery pokes its way into poems, stories, histories and parables. From the romantic "Like a lily among the thorns, So is my darling among the maidens" (Song 2:2 NASB) to the threatening "I will thrash your bodies with the thorns of the wilderness," (Judg 8:7), Bible writers find varied uses for such imagery, but their references to thorns are always negative. Other writers capitalize on thorns' worthlessness, using them as metaphor for that which needs to be discarded or burned: "Every one of them will be thrust away like thorns" (2 Sam 23:6 NASB); "They were extinguished as a fire of thorns" (Ps 118:12 NASB); Like tangled thorns . . . they are consumed (Nah 1:10); and "if it yields thorns ... it ends up being burned" (Heb 6:8 NASB). Some passages accentuate the negative aspects of thorns by associating them with thistles (Gen 3:18), snares (Prov 22:5), nettles (Prov 24:31) and briers (Isa 32:13). Other texts reference thorns when mentioning punishment or *torture: "As pricks in your eyes and as thorns in your sides" (Num 33:55 NASB); "And the soldiers wove a crown of thorns and put it on [Jesus'] head" (John 19:2 NASB);

> and finally Paul's "thorn in the flesh" (2 Cor 12:7) to symbolize his personal torment.
>
> It is significant to note that thorns are in some cases associated with the judgment of Israel's exile. Thus in Isaiah we read that Israel, God's vineyard, will be overgrown with "briers and thorns" (Isa 5:5-6) and "all the land will be briers and thorns" (Isa 7:23-25 NRSV; cf. Isa 32:13; Ezek 28:24; Hos 9:6; 10:8). Here perhaps is an echo of the condition that befalls Adam when he and Eve are exiled from the Garden (Gen 3:18). When Jesus in his parable speaks of some seed being sown among thorns (Mark 4:18-19 and par.), he may have in mind the continuing condition of Israel being in spiritual exile despite its return to the land.[21]

Thorns are like the enemy that arose against Israel (Joshua 23:13). Thorns also represent a life without order and a life without purpose and care (Proverbs 15:19; 24:31). Thorns describe the path of the perverse (Proverbs 22:5). Sinful people are like thorns (Isaiah 33:12; Jeremiah 12:13). Thorns represent financial ruin; thistles will replace their silver and thorns shall destroy their tents (Hosea 9:6). Hosea described the desolation of the backslider like an altar that has been overgrown with thorns (Hosea 10:8). Jesus said the cares of life that choke out the spiritual man are thorns. And Paul described the messenger sent from Satan as a thorn.

The Roman soldiers took this symbol of pain, evil, destruction, desolation, and worldliness and put it on the head

---

[21] *Dictionary of Biblical Imagery.*

of Jesus. Again, nothing was done by accident. The Lord had hardened the heart of Pharaoh, and the Lord caused these soldiers to consider a crown of thorns as a gesture of further mockery. This was done for great significance.

The Curse

To begin, we need to go back to the Fall in the garden. Like much of what we have studied regarding the cross, it all goes back to Genesis. The Lamb of God was slain from the foundation of the world (Revelation 13:8). In other words, the details of the crucifixion were in the mind of God from the very beginning, especially at the curse.

> *And unto Adam he said, Because thou hast hearkened unto the voice of thy wife, and hast eaten of the tree, of which I commanded thee, saying, Thou shalt not eat of it: cursed is the ground for thy sake; in sorrow shalt thou eat of it all the days of thy life;* ***thorns also and thistles shall it bring forth to thee****; and thou shalt eat the herb of the field* (Genesis 3:17-18, emphasis mine).

After Adam and Eve fell into sin. God addressed the situation with harsh judgment. God cursed man, woman, the serpent, and the earth. The evidence of the curse was hardship, pain, and, of course, thorns. The earth would produce thorns as a constant reminder of the sting of sin and pain brought upon mankind by the original sin.

Thorns would the very symbol of the curse of sin. And thorns are what the Roman soldiers fastened upon the head of Jesus. Jesus bore the curse of sin upon His head, and then He took it and nailed it to His cross (Colossians 2:14-15). "Christ hath redeemed us from the curse of the law, ***being made a curse for us***: for it is written, Cursed is every one that hangeth on a tree" (Galatians 3:13, emphasis mine). Everything that Jesus took to Calvary was swallowed up in victory. The curse was rendered completely useless and of no effect.

See Matthew Henry's notes on Matthew 27.

> They platted a crown of thorns, and put it upon his head, v. 29. This was to carry on the humour of making him a mock-king; yet, had they intended it only for a reproach, they might have platted a crown of straw, or rushes, but they designed it to be painful to him, and to be literally, what crowns are said to be figuratively, lined with thorns; he that invented this abuse, it is likely, valued himself upon the wit of it; but there was a mystery in it.
>
> [1.] Thorns came in with sin, and were part of the curse that was the product of sin, Gen 3:18. Therefore Christ, being made a curse for us, and dying to remove the curse from us, felt the pain and smart of those thorns, nay, and binds them as a crown to him (Job 31:36); for his sufferings for us were his glory. [2.] Now he answered to the type of Abraham's ram that was caught in the thicket, and so offered up instead of Isaac, Gen 22:13. [3.] Thorns signify afflictions, 2 Chron 33:11. These Christ put into a crown; so much did he alter the property of them to them that are his, giving them cause to glory in tribulation, and making it to work for them a weight of glory. [4.] Christ was crowned with thorns, to show that his kingdom was not of this world, nor

the glory of it worldly glory, but is attended here with bonds and afflictions, while the glory of it is to be revealed. [5.] It was the custom of some heathen nations, to bring their sacrifices to the altars, crowned with garlands; these thorns were the garlands with which this great Sacrifice was crowned.

[6.] these thorns, it is likely, fetched blood from his blessed head, which trickled down his face, like the previous ointment (typifying the blood of Christ with which he consecrated himself) upon the head, which ran down upon the beard, even Aaron's beard, Ps 133:2. Thus, when he came to espouse to himself his love, his dove, his undefiled church, his head was filled with dew, and his locks with the drops of the night, Song 5:2.[22]

Cursed Earth

I have often wondered why the earth was cursed. I understand the man, for he was the one who sinned. I get the woman; she was the one who convinced Adam to sin. And I certainly understand the serpent. But what did the earth do to deserve a curse? If we look closely, we will discover that the earth has much to do with mankind.

> *And the LORD God formed man of the* ***dust of the ground****, and breathed into his nostrils the breath of life; and man became a living soul* (Genesis 2:7, emphasis mine).

---

[22]Henry, *Commentary on the Whole Bible.*

The earth is substance of man's origin. Every element that makes up the human body can be traced back to the earth. The Bible tells us that God formed Adam from the dirt of the earth. First Corinthians 15:47 says that Adam is from the earth, earthy, and we are a reflection of that earthy substance. Our very nature is corrupted. Paul admonished us to: "Put to death, therefore, whatever belongs to your earthly nature" (Colossians 3:5, NIV). The place that we originated and the place where we will go when we die is a cursed thing. God gives the reason why He cursed the earth in Genesis 3.

> *Both thorns and thistles it shall bring forth for you, and you shall eat the herb of the field. In the sweat of your face you shall eat bread till you return to the ground, for out of it you were taken; for dust you are, and to dust you shall return* (Genesis 3:18-19, NKJV).

Cursed is the earth because it is the source of man's nature. We came from the earth, and when we die, we will return to the ground. A cursed earth birthed us and a cursed earth receives us again. Mankind is cursed coming and going.

> *If there is a natural body, there is also a spiritual body. So it is written: "The first man Adam became a living being"; the last Adam, a life-giving spirit. The spiritual did not come first, but the natural, and after that the spiritual. The first man was of the dust of the earth; the second man is of heaven. As was the earthly man, so are those who are of the earth; and as is the man from heaven, so also are those who are of heaven. And just as we have borne the likeness of the earthly man, so*

> *shall we bear the image of the heavenly man* (I Corinthians 15:44-49, NIV).

Here Paul described for us that we all need to be born again, not of the corruptible earth but of the incorruptible Spirit. (See I Peter 1:23-25.) Jesus told us that anyone who is born of the flesh (earthy nature) cannot enter the kingdom of God. (See John 3:5.) In Paul's teaching, we see the same message: "I declare to you, brothers and sisters, that flesh and blood cannot inherit the kingdom of God, nor does the perishable inherit the imperishable" (I Corinthians 15:50, NIV)

Since Jesus took our curse to the cross and rendered it dead, those who are born again have escaped the corrupted nature of our original state. Even though we are still made of earthly elements and even though we may go back into the earth when we die, the curse of the earth that was instituted in the Garden of Eden will not affect us because Jesus took our cursed earth to the cross.

> *Listen, I tell you a mystery: We will not all sleep, but we will all be changed—in a flash, in the twinkling of an eye, at the last trumpet. For the trumpet will sound, the dead will be raised imperishable, and we will be changed. For the perishable must clothe itself with the imperishable, and the mortal with immortality. When the perishable has been clothed with the imperishable, and the mortal with immortality, then the saying that is written will come true: "Death has been swallowed up in victory." "Where, O death, is your victory? Where, O death, is your sting?" The sting of death is sin, and the power of sin is the law. But thanks be to God! He gives us the*

> *victory through our Lord Jesus Christ.* (I Corinthians 15:51-57, NIV).

The Victor's Crown

A crown represents authority, headship, and dominance. The image of a crown is most recognizable as worn by a king. Kings wear crowns that represent their kingdoms. When one king steps down, he transfers the king's crown to the succeeding king. The crown remains the same from one king to the next. The crown, therefore, will empower whoever wears it to have dominion and authority over everything under that crown's kingdom.

So when a kingdom is conquered by an opposing force, the fallen king must surrender his crown to the victor.

> Possession of a *king's crown by another connotes the usurpation of that king's power. In 2 Sam 1:10 an Amalekite reports to David that he killed Saul. As proof he brings to David Saul's crown and armband. David responds by mourning for Saul, since he considered it unlawful to kill the Lord's anointed. Such restraint against his Israelite rival may be contrasted to 2 Sam 12:30, where David accepts the crown of the defeated king of Rabbah, thus symbolizing the transference of power to David.[23]

At David's triumph over the Ammonites, he took the golden crown of their king and wore it in the presence of all

---

[23] *Dictionary of Biblical Imagery.*

the people. In this instance, David proclaimed the victory over the enemy by taking into his possession the very crown of the Ammonite kingdom. By placing the Ammonite crown upon his head, David thus proclaimed himself the sole victor over the fallen kingdom. David, assuming the crown, became king over the fallen king. Everything in the Ammonite kingdom belonged to David. All of the people, all of the property, all of the spoils, everything was under David's dominion and power, symbolized by placing the crown in his head.

The thorns represented a cursed earth. But when the Romans made it into a crown, it became more than just thorn branches. When they fastened it into a crown, it became the figure of dominion and authority over the curse of sin. It was the crown of a fallen world, and Satan is the king (ruler) of this world. He is the ruler of sinful people.

> *In whom* ***the god of this world*** *hath blinded the minds of them which believe not, lest the light of the glorious gospel of Christ, who is the image of God, should shine unto them* (II Corinthians 4:4, emphasis mine).

The whole world lies under the power of Satan (I John 5:19). The devil tried to tempt Jesus with his kingdom.

> *And the devil, taking him up into an high mountain, shewed unto him all the kingdoms of the world in a moment of time. And the devil said unto him, All this power will I give thee, and the glory of them: for that is delivered unto me; and to whomsoever I will I give it* (Luke 4:5-6).

The crown of thorns represented the kingdom of Satan.

We go back to the promise made at the garden. "And I will put enmity between thee and the woman, and between thy seed and her seed; ***it shall bruise thy head*** " (Genesis 3:15a, emphasis mine). Jesus was going to crush the devil's headship, remove him from authority, and render him a defeated king of a fallen kingdom. When Jesus took the crown of the cursed kingdom, like His predecessor king David, Jesus took dominion and authority over everything in that kingdom. We see the crown of thorns as a sign of shame but it truly became the crown of victory.

As Jesus took the crown, the kingdom of the devil was overthrown and his rule ended. Jesus took possession of everything on earth. All of the spoils are God's. Everything that the enemy had stolen from God was restored to its original owner. Look at how Paul described it in Colossians:

> *For he has rescued us from the dominion of darkness and brought us into the kingdom of the Son he loves, in whom we have redemption, the forgiveness of sins. The Son is the image of the invisible God, the firstborn over all creation. For by him all things were created: things in heaven and on earth, visible and invisible, whether thrones or powers or rulers or authorities; all things have been created through him and for him. He is before all things, and in him all things hold together. And he is the head of the body, the church; he is the beginning and the firstborn from among the dead, so that in everything he might have the supremacy. For God was pleased to have all his fullness dwell in him, and through him to reconcile to himself all things, whether things on earth or things in heaven, by making*

> *peace through his blood, shed on the cross.* (Colossians 1:13-20) NIV.

It is interesting to note that when the devil tempted Jesus, the devil quoted a verse of the Old Testament.

> *And he brought him to Jerusalem, and set him on a pinnacle of the temple, and said unto him, If thou be the Son of God, cast thyself down from hence: for it is written, He shall give his angels charge over thee, to keep thee: and in their hands they shall bear thee up,* ***lest at any time thou dash thy foot against a stone*** (Luke 4:9-11, emphasis mine).

The devil obviously did not understand that the verse he quoted was a prophecy of the Messiah crushing the headship of the devil's kingdom. The original reads in full:

> *For he shall give his angels charge over thee, to keep thee in all thy ways. They shall bear thee up in their hands, lest thou dash thy foot against a stone. Thou shalt tread upon the lion and adder: the young lion and the dragon shalt thou trample under feet* (Psalm 91:11-13).

This psalm holds a promise, for the angels would not allow Jesus to fall to His death prematurely but kept Him so that His heel would not suffer the blow of the stone. Rather, He would render a fatal blow to the head of the lion, the snake, the great dragon himself (the devil) and trample him under His feet.

Jesus came to set the captive free and to restore us to a rightful position within the kingdom of God. He has come to destroy the works of Satan and to deliver us from the bonds of sin.

The devil has stolen our holiness. . . . God took it back.
The devil has taken our dignity. . . . God took it back.
The devil has taken our righteousness. . . . God took it back.
The devil has taken our worship. . . . God took it back.
The devil stole our position of power. . . . God took it back.
The devil wasted us and killed us. . . . God saved us and made us alive and did it while crushing the head of our adversary by taking his crown and placing it on His own head. "Be of good cheer; I have overcome the world," and I wear the victor's crown (John 16:33).

> *And God placed all things under his feet and appointed him to be head over everything for the church, which is his body, the fullness of him who fills everything in every way* (Ephesians 1:22-23, NIV).

Chapter Eleven

The Whole Armor of God

And he saw that there was no man, and wondered that there was no intercessor: therefore his own arm brought salvation unto him; and his righteousness, it upheld him. And he put on righteousness as a breastplate, and a helmet of salvation upon his head; and he put on garments of vengeance for clothing, and was clad with zeal as a mantle. According to their deeds, accordingly he will repay, wrath to his adversaries, recompense to his enemies; to the islands he will repay recompense. So shall they fear the name of Jehovah from the west, and his glory from the rising of the sun; for he will come as a rushing stream, which the breath of Jehovah driveth. And a Redeemer will come to Zion, and unto them that turn from transgression in Jacob, saith Jehovah (Isaiah 59:16b-20).

As noted previously, Isaiah 59 begins with an answer to what seems to be a question posed by fallen humanity, which must have been, "Lord, why have You forsaken us? Is Your hand too weak to save, or is Your hearing too dull to hear our cry?" Through the first fifteen verses, the prophet explained the issue is not with God's power or His hearing. Rather, our sinful nature has separated us from God. We pick up here at verse 16, where God acknowledges the fact that there is no man capable of interceding for a lost humanity.

> He saw that there was no man. Whom is this spoken of, but of Jesus? Who was it saw the poverty and ruin of our nature, and determined to interpose for our salvation, but the Lord Jesus? Who, but he, could be both our Saviour and Intercessor? Precious Lord Jesus! it was, indeed, thine own arm that brought salvation; for the sins of thy people would have crushed every arm but thine, when, in the days of thy flesh, thou didst bear all the sins of thy redeemed in thine own body, on the tree! Oh! how truly lovely is it now, to behold thee, by faith, standing forth, the devoted head of thy body, the Church, and for her enduring the cross, and despising the shame! Oh! how truly blessed, to behold thee in thy priestly garments, and in a vesture dipped, in blood, triumphing over all the power of hell; and in our nature recompensing fury to thine enemies, and manifesting favor to thy chosen! And surely thy zeal to thy Father's house, and to thy Father's honour, may well, from the completeness of it, be compared to the covering of a cloke.[24]

---

[24]*Hawker's Poor Man's Commentary*. Biblesoft Formatted Electronic Database. Copyright © 2014 by Biblesoft, Inc. All rights reserved.

God saw that no man was worthy to be the mediator between sinful man and the holy God. Again, no man could cure the separation issue. So by providence of grace, God came and became our mediator. John was given a similar vision in Revelation.

> *And I saw a strong angel proclaiming with a loud voice, Who is worthy to open the book, and to loose the seals thereof? And no man in heaven, nor in earth, neither under the earth, was able to open the book, neither to look thereon. And I wept much, because no man was found worthy to open and to read the book, neither to look thereon. And one of the elders saith unto me, Weep not: behold, the Lion of the tribe of Juda, the Root of David, hath prevailed to open the book, and to loose the seven seals thereof. And I beheld, and, lo, in the midst of the throne and of the four beasts, and in the midst of the elders, stood a Lamb as it had been slain* (Revelation 5:2-6a).

The Lamb slain was the image of Jesus Christ, God in His fleshly manifestation. "For there is one God and one Mediator between God and men, the Man Christ Jesus" (I Timothy 2:5, NKJV).

Jesus Faced Death Alone

Jesus, as a man, had to face the reality of Calvary alone. At the Garden of Eden the first Adam forsook the will of God and lusted after the will of his own desires. And also at a garden the last Adam forsook His own desires and took upon Himself the will of God. "When Jesus had spoken these words, he went forth with his disciples over the brook Cedron, where was a garden, into the which he entered, and his disciples" (John 18:1). Matthew Henry said of this verse:

> That he entered into a garden. This circumstance is taken notice of only by this evangelist, that Christ's sufferings began in a garden. In the garden of Eden sin began; there the curse was pronounced, there the Redeemer was promised, and therefore in a garden that promised seed entered the lists with the old serpent. Christ was buried also in a garden. (1.) Let us, when we walk in our gardens, take occasion thence to meditate on Christ's sufferings in a garden, to which we owe all the pleasure we have in our gardens, for by them the curse upon the ground for man's sake was removed. (2.) When we are in the midst of our possessions and enjoyments, we must keep up an expectation of troubles, for our gardens of delight are in a vale of tears.[25]

> *And he was withdrawn from them about a stone's cast, and kneeled down, and prayed, saying, Father, if thou be willing, remove this cup from me: nevertheless not my will, but thine, be done. And there appeared an angel unto him from heaven, strengthening him. And being in an agony he prayed more earnestly: and his sweat was as it were great drops of blood falling down to the ground* (Luke 22:41-44).

---

[25]Henry, *Commentary on the Whole Bible.*

In the Garden of Gethsemane our Lord drank, to the dregs, the cup of bitterness. In this place His passion began. The suffering began in prayer. Some have noted that the hardship Jesus faced must have been the knowledge of the tremendous pain that His human body would endure, while others have said that Jesus' agony at Gethsemane must have been caused by the fact that Jesus would become separated from the Spirit of God. Maybe it was all of the above. For us to try to comprehend what must have been overtaking our Lord at this moment would be an impossible task. We could only imagine what it must have been like for Him to face the horror of the ages.

First were the thoughts of taking the sins of the world. A man who knew no sin would have to take upon Himself *all* sin. The thought of this must have been overwhelming. Then add to that the knowledge that Jesus, who had always known the holy presence of the Spirit of the Father with Him, would soon feel the bitterness of separation. The first Adam experienced this horror in the Garden of Eden, and it caused great fear to come over him. Jesus had to face this as well. Then there was the anticipation of physical pain and suffering. The highest level of pain known to man was through the nails. But Jesus had to endure two levels of suffering. The scourging at the whipping post would have been enough trauma to kill some men as the cat of nine tails ripped away the flesh and exposed the bones of His ribs.

Facing the chambers of death alone would be enough to make any man tremble with anxiety. At this moment Jesus had to face the greatest temptation of His life, to throw in the towel. The stress of knowing all of this was almost more than Jesus could bear in the flesh. Medical experts attest that under severe stress, the capillaries in the forehead could burst and produce blood mixed with sweat. Christ was near physical death as He faced the atrocities ahead.

The dreadful part the Lord fell under, and which brought him to the ground in agonies and prayer, was, the frowns of Heaven; in the curse he bore, and the Father's judgment due to sin in consequence of it. The Holy Ghost hath in one short verse described it, and none but God the Holy Ghost could describe it: when under the Spirit of prophecy, Jesus said, Thy rebuke hath broken my heart! Ps 69:20. It is impossible in our researches on this subject to go very far. We know that the curse pronounced on the fall was, In the sweat of thy face shalt thou eat bread. Gen 3:19. But, in sustaining this curse, who would have concluded, that a bloody sweat should follow? All men, more or less, taste of the fruit of Adam's sin, and not only the laboring part eat bread in the sweat of the brow; but the rich and the mighty, some way or other, know the bitterness of it. But while the earth brings forth thorns to all, Jesus only was crowned with them. While men sweat in sorrow, Jesus only sweats a bloody sweat. Precious Lord! in all things thou must bare the pre-eminence! Col 1:18. I have, in the best manner I am able, noticed the different terms the Evangelists make use of concerning Christ's agony in the garden of Gethsemane. See Matt 26:38. He calls it the soul of Christ being exceeding sorrowful even unto death. Mark expresses it, being sore amazed, and very heavy. Mark 14:34. And Luke renders it agony, as one that was at strife, for such is the original. And yet Christ was alone. What strife then could this

> be? Nay, who shall answer the question. An angel appeared from heaven to strengthen him. An angel! Did He who was the image of the invisible God, and with whom it was no robbery to be equal with God, need aid from his creatures? So the word of truth states it; but who is competent to explain a fact so mysterious. Reader! ponder well the subject. Angels desire to look into it. 1 Peter 1:19. surely never, never was there a period in all the annals of mankind, since time began to be numbered, (the cross of Christ excepted, and this was but the close to it) of equal moment with this soul conflict of Christ in the garden of Gethsemane![26]

The curse in the Garden of Eden was that by the sweat of his brow man would accomplish his work (Genesis 3:19). Jesus took upon Himself every curse imposed upon mankind. Only for this last Adam, the work that Jesus was called to do would cause Him to sweat drops of blood. The source of this stress is not mentioned in Scripture. Did Jesus have another bout with Satan, or was He fighting the flesh within? Many speculate about this, but the truth is, no matter the source of the temptation, Jesus needed supernatural strength from heaven. And God gave it to Him.

The Armor of God

Isaiah 59:17 tells us that God would strengthen the Messiah with the armor of God. "And he put on righteousness

---

[26] *Hawker's Poor Man's Commentary.*

as a breastplate, and an helmet of salvation upon his head; and he put on garments of vengeance for clothing, and was clad with zeal as a cloke." As the Lord faced the greatest calamity of human history, God upheld Him with His arm and clothed Him with heavenly armor. This was also prophesied.

> *For he shall give his angels charge over thee, to keep thee in all thy ways. They shall bear thee up in their hands, lest thou dash thy foot against a stone. Thou shalt tread upon the lion and adder: the young lion and the dragon shalt thou trample under feet* (Psalm 91:11-13).

In supplication of prayer the Lord was given the ability to overcome every fear of Cavalry.

Armor is used for fighting battles for hand-to-hand combat. Jesus went into battle for us. He crossed enemy lines to enter the capital city of our adversary. He went to the cross as a Lamb, but He went to battle as the Lion from the tribe of Judah (Revelation 5:5). No warrior, expecting to win, approaches the battlefield without wearing the garments of war, a shield, a sword, and all the protective coverings.

This battle over death, hell, and the grave was no ordinary battle. This battle was not waged upon a physical landscape. The powers He needed to defeat were powers of darkness, fear, and anxiety . . . the rulers of the air. Fitted with spiritual armor to overcome every temptation, no matter the source, Jesus could guard His heart, His head, His hands, and His feet. Without it, He would surely have perished and His heel would have missed the mark of Satan's head and fatally hit the stone instead (Psalm 91:11). This armor allowed Jesus to walk out of death undefeated, covered in the blood of our enemy. (See Isaiah 63:1-6.)

Put on the Whole Armor of God

> *Finally, my brethren, be strong in the Lord and in the power of His might. Put on the whole armor of God, that you may be able to stand against the wiles of the devil. For we do not wrestle against flesh and blood, but against principalities, against powers, against the rulers of the darkness of this age, against spiritual hosts of wickedness in the heavenly places. Therefore take up the whole armor of God, that you may be able to withstand in the evil day, and having done all, to stand. Stand therefore, having girded your waist with truth, having put on the breastplate of righteousness, and having shod your feet with the preparation of the gospel of peace; above all, taking the shield of faith with which you will be able to quench all the fiery darts of the wicked one. And take the helmet of salvation, and the sword of the Spirit, which is the word of God; praying always with all prayer and supplication in the Spirit, being watchful to this end with all perseverance and supplication for all the saints* (Ephesians 6:10-18, NKJV).

When Jesus overcame the world, He ascended into heaven, led captivity captive, and gave gifts to men. These gifts included many things, including the spoils of war.

> Gave gifts unto men—in the psalm, 'thou hast received gifts among men;' i.e., to distribute among men. As a triumphing conqueror

> distributes the spoils of foes as donatives among his people, so Christ, after his conquest of the powers of darkness. The impartation of the gifts of the Spirit depended on Christ's ascension (John 7:39; 14:12). Previous gifts of the Spirit were but an earnest of Pentecost (Acts 2:33). Paul stops short in the middle of the verse, not quoting, 'That the Lord God might dwell among them.' This, though partly fulfilled in Christians being "an habitation of God through the Spirit" (Eph 2:22), ultimately refers (Ps 68:16) to 'the Lord dwelling in Zion forever;' the ascension amidst attendant angels having as its counterpart the second advent amidst "thousands of angels" (Ps 68:17), accompanied by the restoration of Israel (Ps 68:22), the destruction of God's enemies, and the resurrection (Ps 68:20-21,23), the conversion of the kingdoms of the world to the Lord at Jerusalem (Ps 68:29-34).[27]

Gifts from the spoils of conquest are only part of what God has given to us, but included in the gifts was apparently the armor that Jesus was cloaked with in order to face the cross. If God gave Jesus treasures, Jesus has left those treasures with us. We are joint-heirs with Jesus (Romans 8:17). This armor was placed on Christ to overcome the world, to beat all temptation of flesh and Satan. And because He has overcome the world, we can overcome the world through the same armor of God. "These things I have spoken unto you, that in me ye might have peace. In the world ye shall have tribulation: but be of good cheer; I have overcome the world"

[27] *Jamieson, Fausset, and Brown Commentary.*

(John 16:33). If Jesus can face the perils of death, the pain of the cross, and the separation from God and not give up or give in . . . there is no temptation that we could ever dream of facing in which the same armor of God cannot sustain us.

> *For no temptation (no trial regarded as enticing to sin), [no matter how it comes or where it leads] has overtaken you and laid hold on you that is not common to man [that is, no temptation or trial has come to you that is beyond human resistance and that is not adjusted and adapted and belonging to human experience, and such as man can bear]. But God is faithful [to His Word and to His compassionate nature], and He [can be trusted] not to let you be tempted and tried and assayed beyond your ability and strength of resistance and power to endure, but with the temptation He will [always] also provide the way out (the means of escape to a landing place), that you may be capable and strong and powerful to bear up under it patiently* (I Corinthians 10:13, AMP).

If this armor can protect and strengthen the man Christ Jesus from the fear of Calvary, what weapon can the enemy forge that will prosper against those likewise covered? I say none (Isaiah 54:17). What arrow can penetrate the shield of faith? What sword can crush the helmet of the salvation of God? If God's own power upholds you, there is nothing you cannot face wearing the cloak of God's holy armor.

- Can depression penetrate it? No.
- Can fear of anything cripple you? No.

- Can anxiety about persecution, death, or powers of darkness cause you to stumble and fall? No.
- Can any trial ever even come close to that of Calvary? Never, not even close.

This is why Paul tells us that when we have done all we can do to stand, we should just keep standing. When we may feel we cannot stand any longer, our stamina is running out, our strength is weak, and our heart is overwhelmed . . . it may be time to head to your closet—your prayer closet, that is—and reach for that old treasure of war. Find the gift that Jesus handed you when you were washed in His blood and filled with His Spirit. Paul said to go ahead and cover yourself with the:

1. Gospel – Which is the power of God unto salvation.
2. Truth – The revelation of the one God in Christ.
3. Righteousness – Given to you at the cross.
4. Faith – Able to ward off the temptation of Satan.
5. The Word of God – Sharper than any two-edged sword.

Praying with all prayer and supplication is what Jesus was doing in the garden when the angels came to strengthen Him, and the formula is the same for us as well. The next time you are praying for God to strengthen you through the storm of life and to cover you with supernatural strength, I wonder if you could imagine Jesus coming out of death's chamber, victorious over every conceivable trial and temptation. And then watch Him remove His holy armor, placing it on you. We need to understand today that the whole armor of God was awarded to us from the victory at the cross.

May we never take for granted the power that we have to overcome the world. Our ability to have a consistent prayer life will determine our effectiveness against the trials of the evil day. No warrior, expecting to win, approaches the battle-field without wearing the garments of war. And no Christian, expecting to win, approaches the spiritual battlefield without a covering of prayer.

Chapter Twelve

The Mystery of the Cross

This book does not serve to exhaust the depths of the power of the cross. In all honesty, I do not believe we have even scratched the surface of this subject. My hope for everyone who reads this book is that you would become inspired to study to even greater depths and to realize even greater revelations. The tentacles of study could stem from dissecting every piece of the armor of God and how it relates to the victory of the cross. Your study could also dive into the study of the hands, feet, and heart of humanity or discovering the multiple types of the crown of thorns. There are many books written by such authors as Daniel Segraves and J. T. Pugh that would serve as great starting places to dig into the subject of the cross, which, I believe, could never be fully exhausted. Paul told Timothy to study the Word to make himself approved before God. We should take this admonition upon ourselves, noting especially how the Word of God relates to the cross. I believe the greater our revelation is about Calvary, the easier it will be for us to conquer the temptations of sin in this present world.

The Mystery of Godliness

The apostle Paul uses the word "mystery" several times in his epistles. When we think of the word "mystery," the first thought that may come to mind is that of an unsolved dilemma, a concept that cannot be explained or one that is incomprehensible. However, Paul used the word "mystery" from the Greek word *musterion*. The definition of this word in context does not indicate some unsolved mystery but rather a mystery that has been revealed.

> In the New Testament it denotes, not the mysterious (as with the Eng. word), but that which, being outside the range of unassisted natural apprehension, can be made known only by divine revelation, and is made known in a manner and at a time appointed by God, and to those only who are illumined by His Spirit. In the ordinary sense a "mystery" implies knowledge withheld; its Scriptural significance is truth revealed. Hence the terms especially associated with the subject are "made known," "manifested," "revealed," "preached," "understand," "dispensation." The definition given above may be best illustrated by the following passage: "the mystery which hath been hid from all ages and generations: but now hath it been manifested to His saints" Col 1:26, RV.[28]

In scripture "mystery" is used to describe God's deep counsels, which had been a secret but now are revealed and are being revealed. The "mystery" is that they are not understood by everyone. They are only revealed to the believer, but to the carnal mind they are still hidden. Many have said that

---

[28] *Vine's Expository Dictionary of Biblical Words*. Thomas Nelson Publishers. Copyright © 1985.

a definitive answer to the Godhead cannot be explained because Paul told Timothy it is a mystery:

> *And without controversy great is the mystery of godliness: God was manifest in the flesh, justified in the Spirit, seen of angels, preached unto the Gentiles, believed on in the world, received up into glory* (I Timothy 3:16).

The prophets of the Old Testament foretold that God would come and save His people from their sins. This was a mystery to all those who read it and even to those who wrote it. But that great mystery has now been revealed to us because we have witnessed the reality of the prophetic words; God was manifested in the flesh, justified in the Spirit, seen of angels, preached unto the Gentiles, believed on in the world, received up into glory. This is not the mystery of godliness but rather the mystery explained (revealed). Each aspect of Paul's description here poses to answer many Old Testament prophecies concerning the redemption of mankind. This text proves to explain that the Godhead is actually no longer a great mystery but stands as a revelation of how God accomplished His ultimate plan. (See John 1:1-14.)

Other Mysteries Revealed

The second mystery Paul referred to is the mystery of iniquity mentioned in II Thessalonians 2:7. This is often translated as the "mystery of lawlessness." This is the opposition to the mystery of godliness. The lawlessness that will be revealed to us in the last days will coincide with the revealing of the Antichrist. Lawlessness is at work and among us already, yet it is being revealed to us more and more as we approach the end of time.

Next we see the mystery of the church in Ephesians 5:32. This is the revelation of the relationship between God and His church. This hidden truth is now revealed through the relationship between a husband and his wife. Fourth is the mystery of Christ as seen in Ephesians 3:4, the revelation of the union between Jews and Gentiles into one body. It has been revealed to us through the gift of the Holy Spirit. This is the earnest of our inheritance and the seal of our redemption. Then there is the mystery of the final restoration of Israel found in Romans 11:25. Paul hoped that the Roman church would not be ignorant of the revelation of this mystery. Through the process of time, Israel will one day be fully restored under Christ. Paul continued to outline events that will take place, ultimately revealing this truth to the world.

Number six is the mystery of the resurrection found in I Corinthians 15:51. This mystery is how we will not all stay dead in our graves but will be changed, in a moment and in the twinkling of an eye. The last trump will sound and the dead in Christ shall rise. Again, Paul said, "Behold, I shew you a mystery," meaning he would reveal to us a great revelation of something that had not been known previously.

The Mystery of the Cross

This book could have appropriately been called "the mystery of the cross," for there are hidden truths about our redemption that were foretold for centuries and have now been revealed through Christ and His cross. The apostles were commissioned to preach this mystery (or revelation of mystery) to the world. Through the foolishness of preaching, the mystery of the cross is now revealed.

> *But we preach Christ crucified, unto the Jews a stumblingblock, and unto the Greeks*

> *foolishness; but unto them which are called, both Jews and Greeks, Christ the power of God, and the wisdom of God. Because the foolishness of God is wiser than men; and the weakness of God is stronger than men* (I Corinthians 1:23-25).

To the Jews the cross appears to be weakness, and to the Gentiles the cross appears to be foolishness. This is a great mystery to the world, "but unto them which are called" the cross is both the power of God and the wisdom of God.

A truth is found at the foot of Calvary that has been hidden through the ages but fully exposed to every believer as we gaze at the horrific tragedy of the cross. The truth is this: what seems to be utter defeat is actually complete victory. The cross and the preaching of the cross are the revelation of the weakness of God.

This truth has confounded men from the very beginning. We saw in previous chapters how Jesus took on sin's curse from the Garden of Eden. Jesus took on the curse of Adam by the sweat of His brow when He prayed in His own Garden of Gethsemane. There Jesus, being the last Adam, would sweat great drops of blood in total anguish of soul. Then we saw how Jesus took on the curse from the earth by wearing upon His head the crown of thorns, the very symbol of the curse. But what about the woman?

> *To the woman He said, I will greatly multiply your grief and your suffering in pregnancy and the pangs of childbearing; with spasms of distress you will bring forth children. Yet your desire and craving will be for your husband, and he will rule over you* (Genesis 3:16, AMP).

The latter part of this curse can be misunderstood. Some may wonder why a woman's desire for her husband would be a curse. However, if we read it in the New Living Translation, we may find an easier interpretation. "And you will desire to control your husband, but he will rule over you." The curse will be in the power struggle over the household. The blissful relationship once realized in the Garden of Eden was now lost in the curse. I have seen many times when a husband and wife come to the Lord and receive the Holy Ghost. This curse is reversed when the man understands his God-given role to lead his family and likewise when the woman understands the power in her submission to that leadership. When the power struggle ends in a relationship, the curse has lost its sting on a marriage. This is the reason why you will see much teaching on the divine order of the family in the church.

I would like to draw your attention to the first part of the curse upon the woman. God told the woman that He would greatly multiply her pain in childbearing and in pregnancy. Here the power of the cross is revealed in weakness and in suffering. Childbearing has been used throughout Scripture to depict many spiritual truths. Isaiah 66 portrays Zion as a woman who travails and gives birth. This meaning is not literal but allegorical in that Zion will be delivered from Babylon after the righteous spend a period of time in waiting and in suffering.

Childbearing is also highlighted in the three great revivalists in Scripture: Samuel, John the Baptist, and Jesus. Samuel and John the Baptist were very much alike in that they both brought Israel out of a severe drought of hearing God's Word. They both were called of God to announce and anoint the king of Israel. They both took a Nazarite vow, and both were born from a barren womb. Hannah prayed and begged God to allow her to have a child, knowing full well that the process of giving birth would bring her much suffering. She, along with Elizabeth, was willing to endure the pain of childbirth in order that revival would come to Israel. And finally, it was through the virgin womb of Mary that our Savior came and brought everlasting revival to a lost world.

Saved in Childbearing

Why was the birth of these men so detailed in Scripture? For this answer this we must go back to the Fall in the Garden.

> *And Adam was not deceived, but the woman being deceived, fell into transgression. Nevertheless she will be* ***saved in childbearing*** *if they continue in faith, love, and holiness, with self-control* (I Timothy 2:14-15, NKJV, emphasis mine).

If you will recall, the curse was to the serpent first; "Because you have done this, you are cursed more than all cattle, and more than every beast of the field; on your belly you shall go, and you shall eat dust all the days of your life." And then God added the promise of salvation coming through the child born from the woman. "And I will put enmity between you and the woman, and between your seed and her Seed; He shall bruise your head, and you shall bruise His heel" (Genesis 3:14-15, NKJV). Immediately after God gave the promise of hope to lost humanity, He turned to the woman and declared that it would be through multiplied sorrow that she would birth this promise. Hope would come from pain and suffering.

This is the first time we see the mystery of the cross revealed in Scripture, that pain and suffering will ultimately bring hope and salvation. This is what Paul meant when he wrote to Timothy that salvation is brought to pass through the process of childbearing.

I have personally seen my wife give birth on five occasions. In all honesty, these five events were pretty traumatic. I mean, when you see a woman giving birth to a child, it certainly does not appear that any good thing is happening. If you have experienced childbirth, whether firsthand or as a spectator, you know what I am talking about. Giving birth is no Sunday at the park. It has been said that a woman must go to death's door just to bring new life into this world. And from what I have seen, this is very true. If we consider the "promise and the curse" given to Eve, we must know that when Eve conceived her first child she must have anticipated that this child would be the one who would crush the head of the serpent and bring salvation back to humanity. As her day of delivery drew closer, Eve must have been looking forward to the hope within her becoming a reality. And then the day came to deliver this child.

No one knows what Eve's first birth was like since Scripture simply does not say. We do know that there was no precedent for what was about to happen. In other words, Eve had no idea how this was going to work. She had never given birth, nor had she ever seen someone giving birth. Fear of the unknown can make any experience more traumatic than it really is. We also know that there was no anesthesia available. Eve faced the first childbirth alone and endured the full force of suffering. We also know that Eve had a promise. Her seed would bring salvation to her and to her husband. Eve must have endured every contraction, every portion of pain, for however long the labor, with the hope that "if I can just endure the suffering, hope will come."

And when her first child did not bring forth the promise, Eve must have believed that it would be her second child . . . and so on. Every woman who gave birth, from the

Fall until Mary, endured the pain of childbearing with a promise of the hope of salvation.

Mary's childbirth must have been similar to that of Eve in that she had been given a promise that this child would be the Holy One. Mary knew that her pain in childbirth really would bring salvation to the world. And for this reason, Mary must have looked toward the pain and suffering with much joy, knowing that her enduring pain would bring salvation to the world. Hebrews 12:2 tells us that Jesus, "for the joy that was set before him endured the cross." How could Jesus look toward the suffering and pain with joy? Because He knew that through the suffering would be birthed great joy.

> *Verily, verily, I say unto you, That ye shall weep and lament, but the world shall rejoice: and ye shall be sorrowful, but your sorrow shall be turned into joy. A woman when she is in travail hath sorrow, because her hour is come: but as soon as she is delivered of the child, she remembereth no more the anguish, for joy that a man is born into the world. And ye now therefore have sorrow: but I will see you again, and your heart shall rejoice, and your joy no man taketh from you* (John 16:20-22).

Jesus, through pain and suffering, gave birth to the church. When Jesus said that we must be born again of the Spirit, He knew that He would endure the pangs of spiritual childbirth in order to make this new birth possible. "For whatsoever is born of God overcometh the world: and this is the victory that overcometh the world, even our faith" (I John 5:4). We are born of the incorruptible Word of God. We have been birthed into new life with Jesus. Jesus took upon

Himself the curse of woman when He endured multiplied sorrows to make a way for us to become born again.

Victory in Every Defeat

The great mystery of the cross can be seen throughout Scripture in many ways. The story of Joseph is a classic example. He was pronounced dead to his father, sold as a slave into Egypt, and spent many years in an Egyptian prison. What seemed to be defeat was actually victory in disguise. After God exalted Joseph in Egypt and allowed him to save his family from certain death by famine, Joseph said to his brothers, "But as for you, ye thought evil against me; but God meant it unto good, to bring to pass, as it is this day, to save much people alive" (Genesis 50:20).

The weakness of God is when by all accounts it appears the enemy is winning, but he is actually being defeated. Pharaoh appeared to be winning as he approached the Israelites at the Red Sea. When Pharaoh thought he was about to win the victory, the seeming weakness of God became the victory of God. This is how God brings victory over and over again. Samson won the victory after he was brought to his knees in defeat. Through the weakness of flesh God brings the spreading of this gospel.

In the foolishness of preaching God brings salvation to the world. The weakness of God is shown as a man, simply an earthen vessel, can preach to the valley of dry bones and somehow, miraculously, connect a divine and holy heaven to a corrupt, sinful earth. When God calls those who are unlearned and ill-equipped to accomplish His greatest works, this is the mystery of the cross. Paul told the Corinthians:

> *And I, brethren, when I came to you, did not come with excellence of speech or of wisdom*

declaring to you the testimony of God. For I determined not to know anything among you except Jesus Christ and Him crucified. I was with ***you in weakness****, in fear, and in much trembling. And my speech and my preaching were not with persuasive words of human wisdom, but in demonstration of the Spirit and of power, that your faith should not be in the wisdom of men but in the power of God. However, we speak wisdom among those who are mature, yet not the wisdom of this age, nor of the rulers of this age, who are coming to nothing.* ***But we speak the wisdom of God in a mystery, the hidden wisdom which God ordained before the ages for our glory,*** *which none of the rulers of this age knew; for had they known, they would not have crucified the Lord of glory. But as it is written: "Eye has not seen, nor ear heard, nor have entered into the heart of man the things which God has prepared for those who love Him." But God has revealed them to us through His Spirit. For the Spirit searches all things, yes, the deep things of God. For what man knows the things of a man except the spirit of the man which is in him? Even so no one knows the things of God except the Spirit of God. Now we have received, not the spirit of the world, but the Spirit who is from God, that we might know the things that have been freely given to us by God. These things we also speak, not in words which man's wisdom teaches but which the Holy Spirit teaches, comparing spiritual things with spiritual. But the natural man does*

> *not receive the things of the Spirit of God, for they are foolishness to him; nor can he know them, because they are spiritually discerned. But he who is spiritual judges all things, yet he himself is rightly judged by no one. For "who has known the mind of the* LORD *that he may instruct Him?" But we have the mind of Christ* (I Corinthians 2, NKJV, my emphases).

This truth has been hidden through the ages but was slowly revealed in the lives of God's chosen people. The mystery of the cross was being revealed through the destruction of the Flood in Noah's day. The force that brought death and destruction was the same force that birthed a new earth, cleansed of all sin. The old sinful world was passed away, and Noah beheld that all things had become new.

Job lost everything and experienced much suffering and pain. Forty-one chapters of the book of Job spell defeat, and then in chapter 42, the sweet savor of victory was won through the fiery trial of Job's faith.

> *Beloved, do not think it strange concerning the fiery trial which is to try you, as though some strange thing happened to you; but rejoice to the extent that you partake of Christ's sufferings, that when His glory is revealed, you may also be glad with exceeding joy* (I Peter 4:12-13, NKJV).

The weakness of God is seen while we know that He can deliver us from suffering, but He chooses not to do so in order to bring victory to us or to His kingdom. God could have spared Paul and Silas from scourging and kept them from being thrown into the Philippian jail. But God chose not to rescue them, in order to bring salvation to the Philippian jailer (Acts 16). Their wounds of defeat were turned into scars of overwhelming victory.

This is the mystery or revelation of the cross working in your life. When all hell seems to be breaking loose in your life, you can sing and praise God because you know that a greater work of triumph is coming to you. In this plan, God shows us the way of peace: peace in the valley, peace in the storm, peace on the mountain, and peace in the calm.

> *For I have learned in whatever state I am, to be content: I know how to be abased, and I know how to abound. Everywhere and in all things I have learned both to be full and to be hungry, both to abound and to suffer need. I can do all things through Christ who strengthens me* (Philippians 4:11-13, NKJV).

I can do all things, suffer all things, and endure all things because I know that God has a plan for my life. Paul said, "In persecution I gain glory, in chastisement I gain godly character, and even in death I gain Christ."

I would love to tell you that, when you give yourself to God, your life will be free from trials and trouble. But this simply is not our reality. In fact, we are promised that in this world we will have trouble. But be of good cheer, for Jesus has overcome the world (John 16:33). And because Jesus has overcome, we shall likewise be overcomers through every test and every trial.

We have been called to bear the cross, for those who are called to be His sons and daughters are given the revelation of the mystery of the cross. We know that we have hope waiting for us on the other side of every trial we face, even the trial of death.

Thanks be unto God for every victory He has brought to us through the cross.

> *But God forbid that I should glory, save in the cross of our Lord Jesus Christ, by whom the world is crucified unto me, and I unto the world* (Galatians 6:14).

66658906R00128

Made in the USA
Lexington, KY
19 August 2017